## Just getting started with FrameMaker?

### Get free FrameMaker training

I've put together a quick course at techcomm.tools/free-fm-training to show you two things:

- Creating documents with FrameMaker will save you and your company money when you work efficiently
- You can easily learn the skills to edit content with unstructured FrameMaker in just a couple of hours

### HTML5 Publishing training

I love finding out about who's reading my book, and the easiest way for me to get to know you is to bribe you with free stuff!

When you visit techcomm.tools/html5 and tell me who you are, you'll get 3 free lessons on HTML5 publishing with FrameMaker. The lessons are part of my larger Digital Publishing with FrameMaker course, but the lessons are more than just an intro into the topic. They give you what you need to produce default output and improve the branding of your digital project.

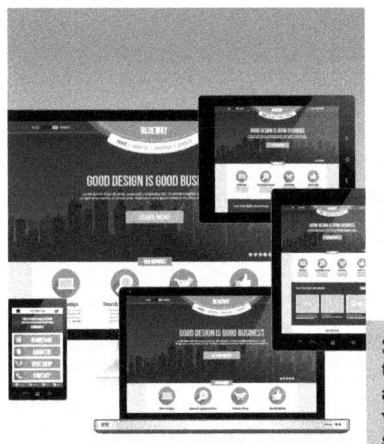

### Need something else?

Tech Comm Tools offers online courses, live classes, and help with specific problems too.

Visit techcommtools.com or see the final page of the book for details.

i

## About the Author

### Matt Sullivan

Matt is the founder of Tech Comm Tools. Along with FrameMaker training and consulting available at www.techcommtools.com, Matt helps organizations deliver content (including video and interactive media within their documentation) to online and mobile users.

Matt is an Adobe Tech Comm Partner, Adobe Certified Trainer, Adobe Certified Expert, and an Adobe Community Professional. He has produced (for Adobe) new feature videos for the past 5 versions of FrameMaker and the Adobe Technical Communication Suite.

He is also the author of

- FrameMaker - Structured Authoring Workbook (2020 Release)
- FrameMaker - Structured Authoring Workbook (2019 Release)
- FrameMaker - Structured Authoring Workbook (2017 Release)
- FrameMaker - Structured EDD Development Workbook (this book, released in 2020)
- FrameMaker - Structured EDD Development Workbook (2019 Release)
- FrameMaker - Structured EDD Development Workbook (2017 Release)
- FrameMaker - Working with Content (2017 Release)
- FrameMaker - Creating and Editing Content (2015 Release)
- Publishing Fundamentals: Unstructured FrameMaker (version 11)

You can find information about print and eBooks of these titles at www.techcommtools.com/books/

Both structured and standard (unstructured) courses are available at www.techcomm.tools/training-courses

Stay up-to-date with #techcomm content by signing up for his free newsletter at www.techcommtools.com/email-list/

Please connect with Matt (*mattrsullivan* on social platforms) and visit the Tech Comm Tools Facebook page at www.facebook.com/tc2ls/

When not working with clients, (and outside of refereeing soccer for Varsity high school, AYSO, and club matches) you'll find Matt surfing and playing beach volleyball with Marianne and his two daughters, or enjoying other things outside.

Reach Matt directly by emailing him at matt@techcommtools.com

# FRAMEMAKER 2020 RELEASE, V16.0.0 STRUCTURED EDD DEVELOPMENT

*A workbook for self-paced or instructor-led training*

Matt R. Sullivan

ISBN: 978-1-953488-00-8

# Important Notice

Copyright 2020 Matt R. Sullivan. All rights reserved.

Portions of this book are used with permission and are copyright © 1997 Adobe Systems Incorporated. All Rights Reserved.

Adobe Systems Incorporated ("Adobe") and its licensors retain all ownership rights to the FrameMaker computer program and other computer programs offered by Adobe (hereinafter collectively called "Adobe Software") and their documentation. Use of Adobe Software is governed by the license agreement accompanying your original media. The Adobe Software source code is a confidential trade secret of Adobe. You may not attempt to decipher, decompile, develop, or otherwise reverse engineer Adobe Software, or knowingly allow others to do so. Information necessary to achieve the interoperability of the Adobe Software with other programs may be available from Adobe upon request. You may not develop passwords or codes or otherwise enable the Save feature of Adobe Software.

This manual, as well as the software described in it, is furnished under license and may only be used or copied in accordance with the terms of such license. The information in this manual is furnished for informational use only, is subject to change without notice, and should not be construed as a commitment by Adobe Systems Incorporated. Adobe Systems Incorporated assumes no responsibility or liability for any errors or inaccuracies that may appear in this book.

Except as permitted by such license, no part of this publication may be reproduced, stored in a retrieval system, or transmitted, in any form or by any means, electronic, mechanical, recording, or otherwise, without the prior written permission of Adobe Systems Incorporated.

Please remember that existing artwork or images that you may desire to scan as a template for your new image may be protected under copyright law. The unauthorized incorporation of such artwork or images into your new work could be a violation of the rights of the author. Please be sure to obtain any permission required from such authors.

Adobe, the Adobe logo, Acrobat, Acrobat Exchange, Adobe Type Manager, ATM, Display PostScript, Distiller, Exchange, Frame, FrameMaker, FrameMaker+SGML, FrameMath, FrameReader, FrameViewer, FrameViewer Retrieval Tools, Guided Editing, InstantView, PostScript, and SuperATM are trademarks of Adobe Systems Incorporated.

APPLE COMPUTER, INC. ("APPLE") MAKES NO WARRANTIES, EXPRESS OR IMPLIED, INCLUDING WITHOUT LIMITATION THE IMPLIED WARRANTIES OF MERCHANTABILITY AND FITNESS FOR A PARTICULAR PURPOSE, REGARDING THE APPLE SOFTWARE. APPLE DOES NOT WARRANT, GUARANTEE OR MAKE ANY REPRESENTATIONS REGARDING THE USE OR THE RESULTS OF THE USE OF THE APPLE SOFTWARE IN TERMS OF ITS CORRECTNESS, ACCURACY, RELIABILITY, CURRENTNESS OR OTHERWISE. THE ENTIRE RISK AS TO THE RESULTS AND PERFORMANCE OF THE APPLE SOFTWARE IS ASSUMED BY YOU. THE EXCLUSION OF IMPLIED WARRANTIES IS NOT PERMITTED BY SOME STATES. THE ABOVE EXCLUSION MAY NOT APPLY TO YOU.

IN NO EVENT WILL APPLE, ITS DIRECTORS, OFFICERS, EMPLOYEES OR AGENTS BE LIABLE TO YOU FOR ANY CONSEQUENTIAL, INCIDENTAL OR INDIRECT DAMAGES (INCLUDING DAMAGES FOR LOSS OF BUSINESS PROFITS, BUSINESS INTERRUPTION, LOSS OF BUSINESS INFORMATION, AND THE LIKE) ARISING OUT OF THE USE OR INABILITY TO USE THE APPLE SOFTWARE EVEN IF APPLE HAS BEEN ADVISED OF THE POSSIBILITY OF SUCH DAMAGES. BECAUSE SOME STATES DO NOT ALLOW THE EXCLUSION OR LIMITATION OF LIABILITY FOR CONSEQUENTIAL OR INCIDENTAL DAMAGES, THE ABOVE LIMITATIONS MAY NOT APPLY TO YOU.

May contain an implementation of the LZW algorithm licensed under U.S. Patent 4,558,302.

The following are copyrights of their respective companies or organizations:

Portions reproduced with the permission of Apple Computer, Inc. © 1997 Apple Computer, Inc.

ImageStream Graphics Filters © 1991-1995 ImageMark Software Labs, Inc. All rights reserved.

Milo © 1988-1995 Ron Avitzur

PANTONE® Computer Video simulation displayed may not match PANTONE-identified solid color standards. Use current PANTONE Color Reference Manuals for accurate color.

"PANTONE Open Color Environment™ (POCE™)"
© Pantone, Inc., 1994.

The spelling and thesaurus portions of Adobe Software are based on THE PROXIMITY LINGUISTIC SYSTEM © 1992 Proximity Technology Inc.; C.A. Stromberg AB; Espasa-Calpe; Hachette; IDE/AS; Kruger; Lluis de Yzaguirre i Maura; Merriam-Webster Inc.; Munksgaard Int. Publishers Ltd.; Nathan; Text & Satz Datentechnik; Van Dale Lexicographie bv; William Collins Sons & Co. Ltd.; Zanichelli. All rights reserved.

The installer software used by the Windows version of this software is based on the Microsoft Setup Toolkit © 1992 Microsoft Corporation.

Portions copyright for the FrameViewer Retrieval Tools © 1988-1995 Verity, Inc. All rights reserved.

The following are trademarks or registered trademarks of their respective companies or organizations:

Microsoft, MS-DOS, Windows / Microsoft Corporation

All other brand or product names are trademarks or registered trademarks of their respective companies or organizations.

Written and designed at Adobe Systems Incorporated, 345 Park Avenue, San Jose, CA 95110 94039-7900, USA

Adobe Systems Europe Limited, Adobe House, 5 Mid New Cultins, Edinburgh EH11 4DU, Scotland, United Kingdom

Adobe Systems Co., Ltd., Yebisu Garden Place Tower, 4-20-3 Ebisu, Shibuya-ku, Tokyo 150, Japan

For defense agencies: Restricted Rights Legend. Use, reproduction, or disclosure is subject to restrictions set forth in subparagraph (c)(1)(ii) of the Rights in Technical Data and Computer Software clause at 252.227-7013.

For civilian agencies: Restricted Rights Legend. Use, reproduction, or disclosure is subject to restrictions set forth in subparagraphs (a) through (d) of the commercial Computer Software Restricted Rights clause at 52.227-19 and the limitations set forth in Adobe's standard commercial agreements for this software. Unpublished rights reserved under the copyright laws of the United States. The contractor/manufacturer is Adobe Systems Incorporated, 345 Park Avenue, San Jose, CA 95110.

# Contents

## Chapter 1: Getting Started

Introduction ........................................................................................ 1
Downloading class files ........................................................................ 1
    *Exercise 1: Downloading class files* ................................................ 1
Understanding How an EDD Controls Structure and Formatting ............. 2
    *Exercise 2: Exploring a raw DTD* ..................................................... 3
    *Exercise 3: Converting a DTD into an EDD* ..................................... 5
    *Exercise 4: Exporting an EDD from a Structured FrameMaker Document* ............. 6
    *Exercise 5: Creating a New EDD from Scratch* .................................. 8
Visualizing a Content Model ................................................................ 9
    *Exercise 6: Analyzing Your Content* ................................................ 10
Hardcopy Sample for Structure Diagram ............................................. 11
Relationship between EDD Elements and their component parts ......... 15
Basic Types of Elements You Can Define ............................................. 16

## Chapter 2: Initial Definition of Your First Element

Introduction ...................................................................................... 17
Setting up your editing environment .................................................. 18
    *Exercise 1: Opening your EDD* ....................................................... 18
    *Exercise 2: Setting Toolbars* ........................................................... 18
    *Exercise 3: Set Elements panel options* ........................................... 19
    *Exercise 4: View Element Boundaries* ............................................. 19
    *Exercise 5: Set New Element Options* .............................................. 20
Specifying an Element Tag .................................................................. 20
    *Exercise 6: Typing the Element Tag* ................................................ 20
Specifying Element Type ..................................................................... 21
    *Exercise 7: Identifying the Element as a Container* ......................... 21
Specifying a ValidHighestLevel Element ............................................. 22
    *Exercise 8: Specifying an element as ValidHighestLevel* ................. 22
Placing Comments in Element Definitions ......................................... 22
    *Exercise 9: Commenting the Element Definition* ........................... 23
Moving forward .................................................................................. 24

## Chapter 3: GeneralRule for Containers and Footnotes

Introduction ...................................................................................... 25
Syntax ................................................................................................ 26
Writing the initial GeneralRules for basic elements ............................ 27
    *Exercise 1: Writing a GeneralRule for a Chapter element* ................ 27
    *Exercise 2: Defining a Title element* ............................................... 28
    *Exercise 3: Defining Section, a container of child elements* ............ 29
    *Exercise 4: Defining More Descendant Container Elements* ........... 30

Importing and Testing ................................................. 31
   *Exercise 5: Importing the EDD* ........................................ 31
   *Exercise 6: Testing the EDD* ......................................... 32
Adding to, modifying, and updating the EDD ............................ 34
   *Exercise 7: Expanding the Section GeneralRule* ........................ 34
   *Exercise 8: Referencing a Group Within a Group* ....................... 35
   *Exercise 9: Reimporting and Retesting* ............................... 35
   *Exercise 10: Referencing an Element Within Itself* .................... 37
   *Exercise 11: Referencing and Defining a Footnote Element* ............. 37

## Chapter 4: GeneralRule for Tables and Table Parts

Introduction .......................................................... 39
Syntax ................................................................ 40
Referencing and Defining the Table Element ............................ 42
   *Exercise 1: Referencing a Table Element in a GeneralRule* ............. 42
   *Exercise 2: Defining a Table Element* ................................ 42
Defining Table Part Elements .......................................... 43
   *Exercise 3: Defining a TableTitle Element* ........................... 43
   *Exercise 4: Defining a TableHeading Element* ......................... 43
   *Exercise 5: Defining a TableBody Element* ............................ 44
   *Exercise 6: Defining a TableFooting Element* ......................... 45
   *Exercise 7: Defining a TableRow Element* ............................. 45
   *Exercise 8: Defining TableCell Elements* ............................. 46
Reimporting and Testing ............................................... 47
   *Exercise 9: Reimporting and Testing the Table* ....................... 47
   *Exercise 10: Testing the Parts of the Table* ......................... 48

## Chapter 5: Tables—InitialStructurePattern and InitialTableFormat

Introduction .......................................................... 51
Specifying an InitialStructurePattern ................................. 52
   *Exercise 1: Specifying the InitialStructurePattern for a TableRow Element* ............. 52
Specifying the InitialTableFormat ..................................... 53
   *Exercise 2: Specifying the InitialTableFormat With an AllContextsRule* ................. 53
Reimporting and Testing ............................................... 53
   *Exercise 3: Reimporting/Testing InitialStructurePattern and InitialTableFormat* ........ 53

## Chapter 6: Inclusions and Exclusions

Introduction .......................................................... 55
Defining Inclusions ................................................... 55
   *Exercise 1: Specifying Inclusions* ................................... 55
Defining Exclusions ................................................... 56
   *Exercise 2: Specifying Exclusions* ................................... 57
Reimporting and Testing Inclusions and Exclusions ..................... 57
   *Exercise 3: Reimporting and Testing Inclusions and Exclusions* ....... 57

## Chapter 7: AutoInsertions

- Introduction .................................................................................. 59
- Specifying Autoinserted Child Elements ............................................ 60
  - *Exercise 1: Specifying Autoinserted Title Element* ........................... 60
  - *Exercise 2: Specifying Autoinserted Head Element* ......................... 60
  - *Exercise 3: Reimporting and Testing Autoinserted Child Elements* ...... 61
- Specifying Autoinserted Child and Nested Child Elements .................. 61
  - *Exercise 4: Specifying Autoinserted Item and Nested Para Elements* .... 61
- Reimporting and Testing Item and Para Autoinsertions ...................... 62
  - *Exercise 5: Reimporting and Testing Autoinserted Nested Child Elements* ............... 62

## Chapter 8: Defining and Formatting Objects

- Introduction .................................................................................. 65
- CrossReference Elements ................................................................ 66
  - *Exercise 1: Defining a CrossReference and InitialObjectFormat* .......... 66
  - *Exercise 2: Reimporting and Testing the Cross-Reference Element* ...... 67
- Equation Elements ......................................................................... 69
  - *Exercise 3: Defining an Equation and Specifying Its InitialObjectFormat* ............... 69
  - *Exercise 4: Reimporting and Testing the Equation Element* ............... 70
- Graphic Elements ........................................................................... 70
  - *Exercise 5: Defining a Graphic and Specifying Its InitialObjectFormat* .... 70
  - *Exercise 6: Reimporting and Testing the Graphic Element* ................ 72
- Marker Elements ............................................................................ 73
  - *Exercise 7: Defining a Marker and Specifying Its InitialObjectFormat* .... 73
  - *Exercise 8: Reimporting and Testing the Marker Element* ................. 74
- SystemVariableFormatRule .............................................................. 75
  - *Exercise 9: Defining a System Variable and Specifying Its Format Rule* ... 75
  - *Exercise 10: Reimporting and Testing the System Variable Element* ..... 76

## Chapter 9: Attribute List

- Introduction .................................................................................. 77
- Basic Types of Attributes and Their Parts .......................................... 78
- Defining attributes for metadata ...................................................... 79
  - *Exercise 1: Defining a Required String Attribute* ............................. 79
  - *Exercise 2: Defining an Optional Real Attribute with a Range and Default* ............ 80
  - *Exercise 3: Reimporting and Testing Attributes* ............................... 81
- Defining Attributes for Prefixes and Formatting ................................. 82
  - *Exercise 4: Defining an optional choice attribute to provide a prefix* ..... 82
  - *Exercise 5: Defining an Optional Choice Attribute to Provide Formatting* ........... 83
  - *Exercise 6: Defining an optional choice attribute to provide InitialObjectFormat* ...... 84
- Defining Attributes for Cross-Referencing ......................................... 85
  - *Exercise 7: Defining an Optional, ReadOnly UniqueID Attribute for a Source* ......... 85
  - *Exercise 8: Defining a Required, ReadOnly IDReference attribute for XRef* .......... 87

## Chapter 10: AllContext formatting rules

Introduction . . . . . . . . . . . . . . . . . . . . . . . . . . . . . . . . . . . . . . . . . . . . . . . . . . . . . . . . . . . . . . . . . . . . . . . . 91
The parts that make up TextFormatRules . . . . . . . . . . . . . . . . . . . . . . . . . . . . . . . . . . . . . . . . . . . . . 92
Specifying the ElementPgfFormatTag . . . . . . . . . . . . . . . . . . . . . . . . . . . . . . . . . . . . . . . . . . . . . . . . 93
    *Exercise 1: Specifying a Base Tag for the Entire Flow* . . . . . . . . . . . . . . . . . . . . . . . . . . . . . 94
Understanding an AllContextsRule . . . . . . . . . . . . . . . . . . . . . . . . . . . . . . . . . . . . . . . . . . . . . . . . . . 94
    *Exercise 2: Specifying an AllContextsRule Referring to "Basic" Properties* . . . . . . . . . . . . . . . 95
    *Exercise 3: Specifying an AllContextsRule Referring to Many Properties* . . . . . . . . . . . . . . . . 96
    *Exercise 4: Specifying an AllContextsRule Referring to a FormatChangeList* . . . . . . . . . . . . . 97
    *Exercise 5: Defining a FormatChangeList* . . . . . . . . . . . . . . . . . . . . . . . . . . . . . . . . . . . . . . . . 98
    *Exercise 6: Specifying a Second AllContextsRule* . . . . . . . . . . . . . . . . . . . . . . . . . . . . . . . . . . 99
    *Exercise 7: Specifying an AllContextsRule Referring to Text-Range Properties* . . . . . . . . . . 99
    *Exercise 8: Formatting Captions with Two Rules* . . . . . . . . . . . . . . . . . . . . . . . . . . . . . . . . . . 100
    *Exercise 9: Formatting TableTitle Text* . . . . . . . . . . . . . . . . . . . . . . . . . . . . . . . . . . . . . . . . . 101

## Chapter 11: ContextRule formatting rules

Introduction . . . . . . . . . . . . . . . . . . . . . . . . . . . . . . . . . . . . . . . . . . . . . . . . . . . . . . . . . . . . . . . . . . . . . 103
Writing a ContextRule . . . . . . . . . . . . . . . . . . . . . . . . . . . . . . . . . . . . . . . . . . . . . . . . . . . . . . . . . . . . 103
ContextRule—Naming Ancestors . . . . . . . . . . . . . . . . . . . . . . . . . . . . . . . . . . . . . . . . . . . . . . . . . . . 103
    *Exercise 1: Specifying a ContextRule with One Clause Naming a Parent* . . . . . . . . . . . . . . . 105
    *Exercise 2: Indenting Lists* . . . . . . . . . . . . . . . . . . . . . . . . . . . . . . . . . . . . . . . . . . . . . . . . . . . 106
    *Exercise 3: Specifying a ContextRule with Two Clauses Naming a Parent* . . . . . . . . . . . . . . 106
ContextRule—Naming Siblings and Naming Attribute Values . . . . . . . . . . . . . . . . . . . . . . . . . . 108
    *Exercise 4: Formatting Paras Using Attribute Values and Sibling Indicators* . . . . . . . . . . . 110
    *Exercise 5: Controlling FrameMaker Behavior Using Attribute Values* . . . . . . . . . . . . . . . . 113
Writing a LevelRule . . . . . . . . . . . . . . . . . . . . . . . . . . . . . . . . . . . . . . . . . . . . . . . . . . . . . . . . . . . . . . 113
    *Exercise 6: Numbering Headings Using LevelRules* . . . . . . . . . . . . . . . . . . . . . . . . . . . . . . . 114
Using Context Labels . . . . . . . . . . . . . . . . . . . . . . . . . . . . . . . . . . . . . . . . . . . . . . . . . . . . . . . . . . . . . 116
    *Exercise 7: Providing ContextLabels for Headings* . . . . . . . . . . . . . . . . . . . . . . . . . . . . . . . . 116
Optional Exercise . . . . . . . . . . . . . . . . . . . . . . . . . . . . . . . . . . . . . . . . . . . . . . . . . . . . . . . . . . . . . . . . 117
    *Exercise 8: Writing a SubRule for Paras in Items in Lists* . . . . . . . . . . . . . . . . . . . . . . . . . . . 117

## Chapter 12: First/LastParagraphRules

Introduction . . . . . . . . . . . . . . . . . . . . . . . . . . . . . . . . . . . . . . . . . . . . . . . . . . . . . . . . . . . . . . . . . . . . . 119
Specifying First/LastParagraphRules . . . . . . . . . . . . . . . . . . . . . . . . . . . . . . . . . . . . . . . . . . . . . . . . 119
    *Exercise 1: Specifying Formatting Properties with First/Last Rules* . . . . . . . . . . . . . . . . . . 119

## Chapter 13: PrefixRules and SuffixRules

Introduction . . . . . . . . . . . . . . . . . . . . . . . . . . . . . . . . . . . . . . . . . . . . . . . . . . . . . . . . . . . . . . . . . . . . . 121
Specifying PrefixRules and SuffixRules . . . . . . . . . . . . . . . . . . . . . . . . . . . . . . . . . . . . . . . . . . . . . . 124
    *Exercise 1: Specifying Prefix Based on Attribute Value* . . . . . . . . . . . . . . . . . . . . . . . . . . . . 124
    *Exercise 2: Specifying Quotation Marks Around a Text-Range Element* . . . . . . . . . . . . . . . 125

## Chapter 14: Elements for Structuring Books

Introduction . . . . . . . . . . . . . . . . . . . . . . . . . . . . . . . . . . . . . . . . . . . . . . . . . . . . . . . . . . . . . . . . . . . . . . . . . . . . . 127
Defining and Testing Book Elements . . . . . . . . . . . . . . . . . . . . . . . . . . . . . . . . . . . . . . . . . . . . . . . . . . . 128
    *Exercise 1: Defining an Element for the Entire Book* . . . . . . . . . . . . . . . . . . . . . . . . . . . . . . . . . 128
    *Exercise 2: Defining Elements for the Generated Files* . . . . . . . . . . . . . . . . . . . . . . . . . . . . . . . 128
    *Exercise 3: Reimporting and Retesting* . . . . . . . . . . . . . . . . . . . . . . . . . . . . . . . . . . . . . . . . . . . . . 129
Generating a FrameMaker Book . . . . . . . . . . . . . . . . . . . . . . . . . . . . . . . . . . . . . . . . . . . . . . . . . . . . . . . 130
    *Exercise 4: Importing the Element Definitions into the Chapter* . . . . . . . . . . . . . . . . . . . . . . . 130
    *Exercise 5: Generating a Book* . . . . . . . . . . . . . . . . . . . . . . . . . . . . . . . . . . . . . . . . . . . . . . . . . . . . 131
    *Exercise 6: Adding Files* . . . . . . . . . . . . . . . . . . . . . . . . . . . . . . . . . . . . . . . . . . . . . . . . . . . . . . . . . . 131
    *Exercise 7: Rearranging Files in the Book* . . . . . . . . . . . . . . . . . . . . . . . . . . . . . . . . . . . . . . . . . . 132
    *Exercise 8: Correcting a NoName Element* . . . . . . . . . . . . . . . . . . . . . . . . . . . . . . . . . . . . . . . . . 132
    *Exercise 9: Updating the book to correct Chapter elements in Structure View* . . . . . . . . . . 133
    *Exercise 10: Adding a Table of Contents* . . . . . . . . . . . . . . . . . . . . . . . . . . . . . . . . . . . . . . . . . . . 134
    *Exercise 11: Adding an index* . . . . . . . . . . . . . . . . . . . . . . . . . . . . . . . . . . . . . . . . . . . . . . . . . . . . . 135
    *Exercise 12: Formatting a Table of Contents* . . . . . . . . . . . . . . . . . . . . . . . . . . . . . . . . . . . . . . . 136
    *Exercise 13: Formatting an Index* . . . . . . . . . . . . . . . . . . . . . . . . . . . . . . . . . . . . . . . . . . . . . . . . . 137
    *Exercise 14: Setting up the Book Files* . . . . . . . . . . . . . . . . . . . . . . . . . . . . . . . . . . . . . . . . . . . . . 138
    *Exercise 15: Update the Book* . . . . . . . . . . . . . . . . . . . . . . . . . . . . . . . . . . . . . . . . . . . . . . . . . . . . 139
    *Exercise 16: Reviewing the Book Files* . . . . . . . . . . . . . . . . . . . . . . . . . . . . . . . . . . . . . . . . . . . . . 140

## Chapter 15: Structuring Unstructured Data

Introduction . . . . . . . . . . . . . . . . . . . . . . . . . . . . . . . . . . . . . . . . . . . . . . . . . . . . . . . . . . . . . . . . . . . . . . . . . . . . . 141
Rule Syntax—Character Restrictions . . . . . . . . . . . . . . . . . . . . . . . . . . . . . . . . . . . . . . . . . . . . . . . . . . . 142
Wildcard character (%) in Tags: . . . . . . . . . . . . . . . . . . . . . . . . . . . . . . . . . . . . . . . . . . . . . . . . . . . . . . . . . 142
Methods for Producing a Conversion Table . . . . . . . . . . . . . . . . . . . . . . . . . . . . . . . . . . . . . . . . . . . . 142
    *Exercise 1: Generating Initial Conversion Table* . . . . . . . . . . . . . . . . . . . . . . . . . . . . . . . . . . . . 142
Typing the Conversion Rules . . . . . . . . . . . . . . . . . . . . . . . . . . . . . . . . . . . . . . . . . . . . . . . . . . . . . . . . . . . 145
    *Exercise 2: Writing Rules for Text Ranges* . . . . . . . . . . . . . . . . . . . . . . . . . . . . . . . . . . . . . . . . . . 147
    *Exercise 3: Writing Rules for Paragraphs* . . . . . . . . . . . . . . . . . . . . . . . . . . . . . . . . . . . . . . . . . . 148
    *Exercise 4: Writing Rules for Footnotes* . . . . . . . . . . . . . . . . . . . . . . . . . . . . . . . . . . . . . . . . . . . . 150
    *Exercise 5: Writing Rules for Cross-References* . . . . . . . . . . . . . . . . . . . . . . . . . . . . . . . . . . . . . 150
    *Exercise 6: Writing Rules for Equations* . . . . . . . . . . . . . . . . . . . . . . . . . . . . . . . . . . . . . . . . . . . . 150
    *Exercise 7: Writing Rules for Graphics* . . . . . . . . . . . . . . . . . . . . . . . . . . . . . . . . . . . . . . . . . . . . . 151
    *Exercise 8: Writing Rules for Markers* . . . . . . . . . . . . . . . . . . . . . . . . . . . . . . . . . . . . . . . . . . . . . . 151
    *Exercise 9: Writing Rules for Tables and Table Parts* . . . . . . . . . . . . . . . . . . . . . . . . . . . . . . . . 152
    *Exercise 10: Wrapping Captions and Graphics in Figures* . . . . . . . . . . . . . . . . . . . . . . . . . . . 153
    *Exercise 11: Wrapping Paras in Items in Lists* . . . . . . . . . . . . . . . . . . . . . . . . . . . . . . . . . . . . . . 154
    *Exercise 12: Wrapping Heads and Their Siblings in Sections* . . . . . . . . . . . . . . . . . . . . . . . . . 155
    *Exercise 13: Wrapping the Highest-Level Element* . . . . . . . . . . . . . . . . . . . . . . . . . . . . . . . . . . 155
Completed Conversion Table . . . . . . . . . . . . . . . . . . . . . . . . . . . . . . . . . . . . . . . . . . . . . . . . . . . . . . . . . . 156
Structuring Unstructured Documents . . . . . . . . . . . . . . . . . . . . . . . . . . . . . . . . . . . . . . . . . . . . . . . . . . 157
    *Exercise 14: Structuring Current Unstructured Document* . . . . . . . . . . . . . . . . . . . . . . . . . . 157

# Chapter 1: Getting Started

## Introduction

In this module, you will learn how FrameMaker works with structured content models, identify how to get started creating an Element Definition Document, identify the various types of elements you can define and the various parts of an element definition.

### Objectives

- Download class files referenced in exercises
- Define structured documentation
- Review overall development process
- Identify several ways to create initial EDD
- Identify basic types of elements you can define
- Identify parts of element definition

## Downloading class files

The first few lessons utilize sample files, and later lessons have incremental files available for your use to help keep you aligned with the workbook.

If class files haven't already been downloaded for your use, you'll want to download them before starting the lessons.

### Exercise 1:  Downloading class files

To download the lesson files:

1. Open a browser like Chrome or FireFox and navigate to **https://techcomm.tools/fm-edd-16-0-0pr**
2. Provide your name and email to get the files sent to you via email. A confirmation message will be sent to ensure you've entered the proper address.
3. Answer the confirmation message in the affirmative to receive the file download link for your file.
4. Decompress the file sent via email to your preferred location. Choose something easy for you to remember and to type (like the root of the C: drive, your desktop, or your Documents folder) as you'll need to navigate to these files throughout the course.

## Understanding How an EDD Controls Structure and Formatting

Structured documents are organized into logical chunks of information, called elements. Elements have rules related to their:

- Content
- Hierarchy
- Order
- Frequency
- Necessity (Required or Optional)

A content model in XML and SGML environments is defined by either a Document Type Definition (DTD) or a Schema. FrameMaker uses a document called an Element Definition Document (EDD) to manage both the content model and the formatting of the content itself.

Authors focus on content and organization of information, not formatting. Focusing on content promotes documentation consistency throughout companies and across industries. Consistency improves communication of information.

In FrameMaker, authors create and edit documents using elements which are:

- Defined in a corresponding EDD
- Imported into design template, creating the element catalog in the design template. The element catalog, along with other traditional FrameMaker components like master pages and other formatting information make up a structured template.

 As of 16.0.0, what is commonly refered to as the Element Catalog is displayed in the Elements panel. These phrases are used interchangeably in this book, at least until Adobe changes the label of either the menu item or the Elements panel.

### Ways to create an EDD

There are several ways to create an initial EDD:

- If you are conforming to an existing DTD, you can convert a DTD to an EDD.
- If no DTD exists, but you have a structured FrameMaker document containing an element catalog, you can export the element catalog as an EDD from your structured document.
- If a schema exists, you can import the schema into FrameMaker as an EDD.
- If no DTD and no comparable structured document, you can start with a new, empty EDD.

After a brief review of DTD and EDD files, you'll start in this workbook with a new, empty EDD.

Chapter 1: Getting Started                                                Exercise 2: Exploring a raw DTD

### Exercise 2: Exploring a raw DTD

In this exercise, you will open a sample DTD, without converting it to an EDD, and view it as a text file.

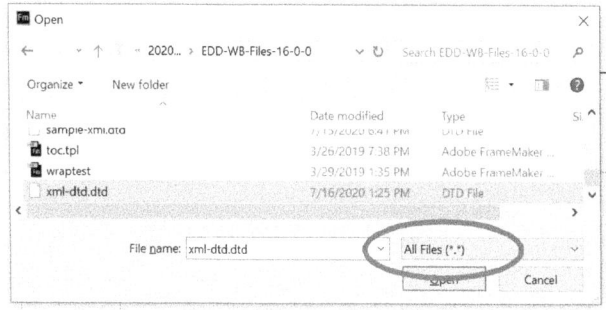

1. From your **EDD-WB-Files-16-0-0a** directory, open **xml-dtd.dtd**.

    a. From the **File** menu, choose **Open**.

       The **Open** dialog appears.

       If necessary, change to your class files directory.

 If necessary, choose **All Files (*.*)** from the filetype menu.

    b. Double-click **xml-dtd.dtd**.

       The **Unknown File Type** dialog appears.

    c. Select **Text** and click **Convert**.

       The **Reading Text File** dialog appears.

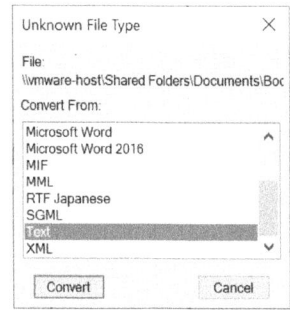

    d. Select **Treat Each Line as a Paragraph** and click **Read**.

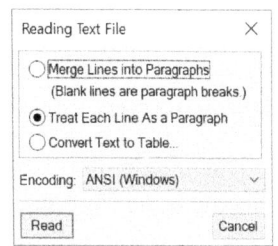

3

The sample DTD appears.

2. Scroll through the DTD, viewing its contents.

```
<!--DTD for Chapter. Typically invoked by
    <!DOCTYPE  Chapter  SYSTEM "c:\class\sample-xml.dtd">
-->

<!--Chapter: Chapter is container of all elements within individual chapter of
 maintenance manual-->
<!ELEMENT Chapter   (Title, Section, Section+) >
<!ATTLIST Chapter   Author    CDATA      #REQUIRED
                    Version   NMTOKEN    "1.0" >

<!ELEMENT Title     (#PCDATA) >
<!ATTLIST Title  ID ID  #IMPLIED >

<!ELEMENT Section   (Head, (((Para, List?)+, (Section, Section+)?) |
                           (Section, Section+))) >

<!ELEMENT Head      (#PCDATA) >
<!ATTLIST Head      ID        ID         #IMPLIED >

<!ELEMENT List      (Item, Item+) >
<!ATTLIST List      ListType  (Bulleted|Numbered)  "Bulleted" >
<!ELEMENT Item      (Para+) >

<!ELEMENT Para      (#PCDATA) >
```

> The text version of the DTD is more like application code, and not very human-friendly.

3. Leave this file open for comparison with the file in the next exercise.

FrameMaker gives you the ability to process

- XML DTDs
- SGML DTDs
- Schema content models

into FrameMaker as unformatted EDDs.

In the next exercise, you will convert a DTD to an EDD, which results in a more readable version of the DTD code.

Chapter 1:   Getting Started                                                      Exercise 3:  Converting a DTD into an EDD

### Exercise 3:   Converting a DTD into an EDD

In this exercise, you will open a sample DTD, converting it to an EDD, and view the resulting element definitions.

1. Select **Structure > DTD > Open DTD**.

    The **Open DTD** dialog appears.

2. If necessary, change to your class files directory.

3. Double-click **xml-dtd.dtd**.

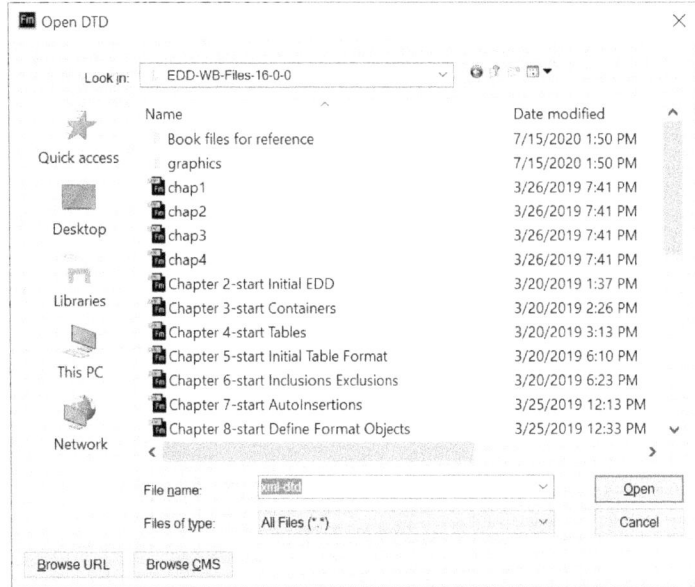

The **Use Structured Application** dialog appears.

4. Choose **<No Application>** from the **Use Structured Application** popup menu, and click **Continue**.

    The **Select Type** dialog appears.

5. Select **XML** (if necessary) and select **OK**.

An alert appears with the message, "Finished reading DTD."

6. Click **OK** to dismiss alert.

    An untitled EDD appears with element and attribute definitions corresponding to original DTD.

7. Scroll through the EDD, viewing its contents.

8. Compare this EDD with the DTD you explored in Exercise 2.

   Note that the EDD is easier to read than the raw DTD.

   Because, you are experimenting with the various ways to create an EDD, there's no need to save this EDD.

9. Close the file without saving.

Next, you will see how to export the element catalog as EDD from a structured document with comparable structure.

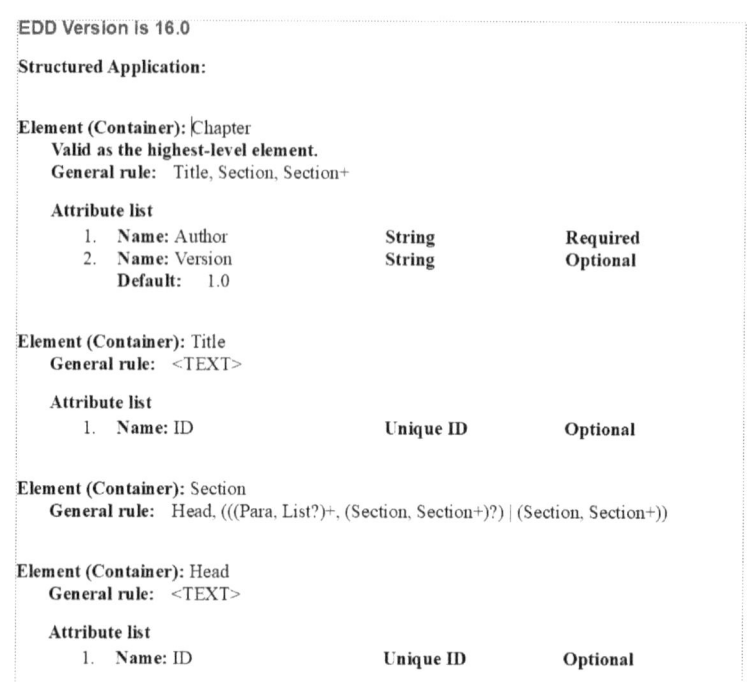

## Exercise 4: Exporting an EDD from a Structured FrameMaker Document

In this exercise, you will export the element catalog as an EDD from a structured document.

1. From your class files directory, open **fm-sample.fm**.

   a. Display the **Open** dialog by choosing **File > Open**.

   b. If necessary, change to your class files directory.

   c. Double-click **sample.fm**. Dismiss any missing resource dialogs.

   The sample structured document appears.

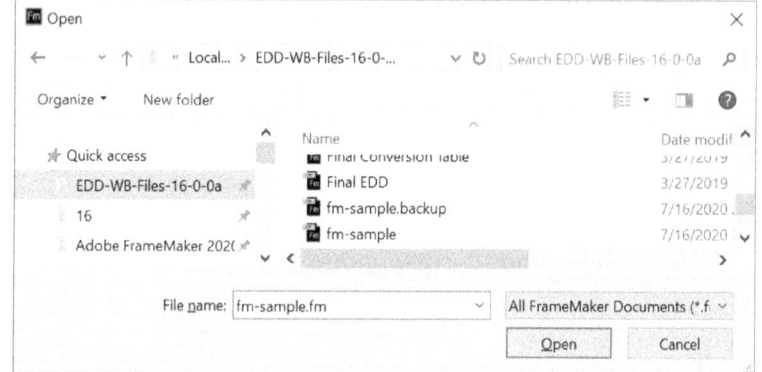

2. Scroll through the sample document, viewing its contents.

3. Choose **Structure > Structure View** to display the **Structure View** pane.

   The **Structure View** displays the document contents in a hierarchy of elements.

4. Choose **View > Panels > Element Catalog** to display the **Elements** panel.

   The **Elements** panel currently displays all the elements available for insertion in this document.

5. Create a new EDD based on the current document's element catalog by choosing **Structure > EDD > Export Element Catalog as EDD**.

   An untitled FrameMaker document appears (an EDD), with the element and attribute definitions corresponding to **Elements** panel of the Sample.fm structured document. Note this document refers to the file from which it was exported.

6. Scroll through the EDD, viewing its contents.

   Take note of the **Structure View** and the elements displayed there.

   Note the addition of formatting specifications in this file.

   Because, you are experimenting with the various ways to create an EDD, you will not save this EDD. Next, you will create an EDD from scratch.

7. Close the EDD without saving.

8. Close the **Sample.fm** document without saving.

Chapter 1: Getting Started     Exercise 5: Creating a New EDD from Scratch

 **Exercise 5:   Creating a New EDD from Scratch**

In this exercise, you will create a new EDD and save it in your Class directory with an appropriate filename.

1. Choose **Structure > EDD > New EDD**.

   The new EDD appears.

   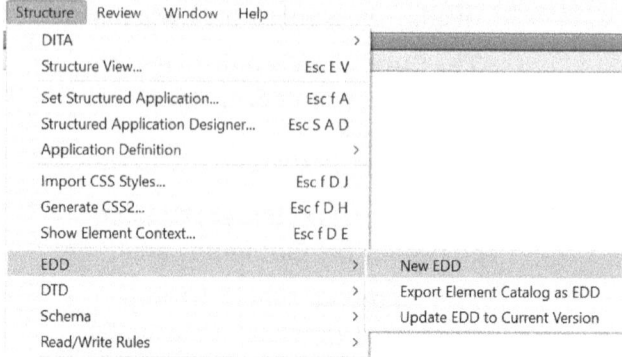

2. If not already open, open the **Structure View** and the **Elements** panel.

   The **Structure View** displays the elements automatically inserted with any new EDD, with the insertion point to the right of the Tag element bubble. If needed, click to the right of the tag element in the **Structure View**.

   The **Elements** panel displays **<TEXT>**, prompting you to type the Tag of the first element you are defining.

   Next, you will save the EDD with the appropriate filename and analyze your document type for its structure, the most important step before beginning to define your elements.

   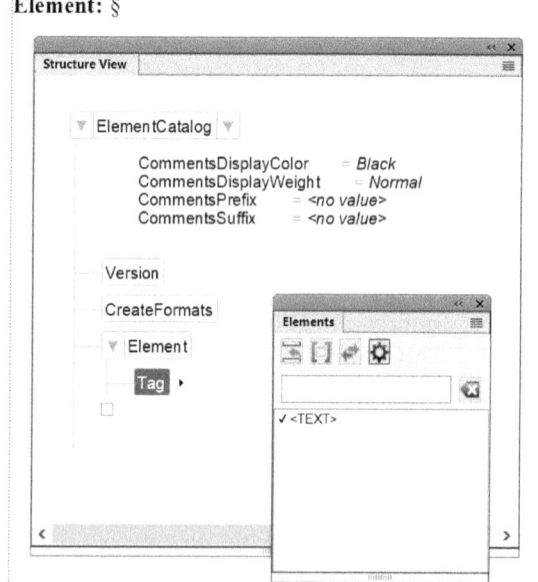

3. Use the **Save As** dialog to save the EDD in the directory containing your class files with the new filename, `EDD.fm`.

   a. From the File menu, choose **Save As**.

      The **Save Document** dialog appears.

   b. If necessary, change to your class files directory.

   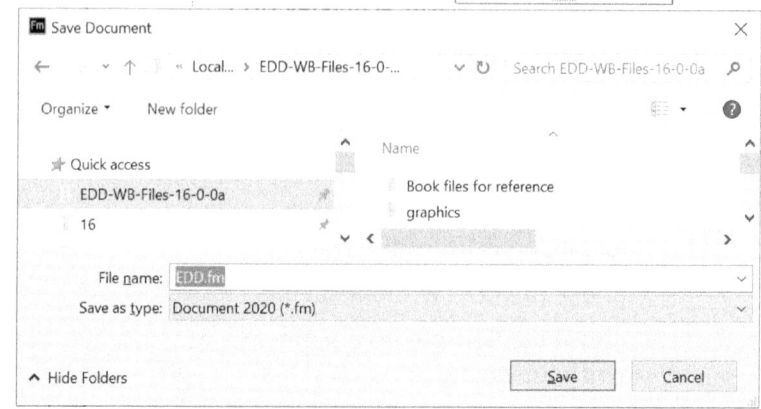

8

c. In the **File name** field, delete the current file name and type: `EDD.fm`
d. Click **Save**.

 If you omit the .fm extension, FrameMaker will automatically add it for you.

# Visualizing a Content Model

Throughout the EDD development in this training course, you will be acting as the structure developer for the publications department of a fictional transit authority. You will ensure that all maintenance manuals written by your department have the same structure.
Throughout the next series of exercises, you will:

- Analyze the document type for its structure
- Define your elements and attributes in an EDD
- Test the element definitions by
    - Importing them into a template
    - Inserting, wrapping, changing, merging, splitting, unwrapping elements
    - Inserting and editing attribute values

When you analyze your document type (in this case, maintenance manuals), you draw a diagram of the document's structure, showing:

- Logical chunks of information, called elements
- Element hierarchy
- Element content
- Element order
- Notations about frequency about whether the elements are required or optional
- Attribute information

The structure diagram can be as minimal or as detailed as you want.
Typically, the more analysis done up front, the easier it will be to define your elements.

When analyzing your content:

- Work as a small team to get input from all those involved in using and approving the structure—authors (end users), format designers, structure developers, managers
- Work with a representative sample of the content
- Incorporate any company specifications—structure or style guides
- Analyze from the top down—bigger chunks first, then smaller chunks as needed
- Provide only as much structure as needed—don't over analyze

If after learning this material you have (or are transitioning to) an existing content model, then the content analysis will have already been completed.
If you will be creating a custom model for your internal use, then the content analysis will be a very important part of your migration project.

**Exercise 6: Analyzing Your Content**

In this exercise, you will analyze your content for its structure, the most important step before beginning to define your elements.

Normally, you would be viewing many samples of chapters, as well as the entire manual. In this set of materials you will start with something simple and enhance its structure as you go along.

1. Review the sample (the next six pages of this module) of a chapter in the maintenance manual for your fictional organization.

    You will finish by defining an entire book with a table of contents and index by the end of the course.

2. Take out a sheet of paper and take about five minutes to map out a diagram of its structure as you see it, similar to the diagram on page 14 in this module.

 Normally, this is an iterative process, involving a team of authors (end users), format designers, structure developers, and managers. It might take hours, if not days or even weeks of revision for more complicated structures.

3. If you are learning this material in a class or course, compare your structure diagram to your neighbor's, noticing the different possibilities for this fairly simple structure. If not, consider how you might alternately represent the content.

4. Compare your structure diagram to the one on page 14, familiarizing yourself with its:
    - Element tags
    - Element hierarchy
    - Element content
    - Element order
    - Notations about frequency and whether the elements are required or optional

Once you're finished with this exercise, review the reference tables at the end of the module. They describe the relationship between different types of elements and their component parts. You may want to refer back to these tables as you go through the material.

# Hardcopy Sample for Structure Diagram

Page 1

## Chapter 1. Side Doors

### 1.1. Introduction

#### 1.1.1. Chapter Overview

##### 1.1.1.1. Procedures in This Chapter

This chapter describes maintenance procedures for the side doors on the AstroLiner T440B and T442 light rail cars. It includes safety guidelines, an overview of door components, and a maintenance schedule for some of the components.

The procedures in this chapter cover disassembling and reinstalling door panels.

##### 1.1.1.2. Related Information

For information about routine operational testing, see *Chapter 5 of the manual Testing and Troubleshooting* in this volume, part number TT1-500 093. For detailed troubleshooting techniques that address specific side door problems, see *Chapter 18 of the same manual*.

Page 2

#### 1.1.2. Safety Guidelines

##### 1.1.2.1. Basic Precautions

All maintenance personnel must wear approved protective clothing and follow the safety guidelines outlined in the *Work Safely booklet* at all times.

##### 1.1.2.2. Additional Safety Measures

Additional safety measures must be observed when working on the electrical and pneumatic systems of the side doors. Follow these rules in particular:

- Turn off all power to high-voltage equipment, and ground all wires before performing maintenance procedures.
- Always work with your assigned "buddy" or another technician present who can perform CPR or call for aid if necessary.

Some of the procedures in this chapter have warnings regarding the hazards associated with specific tasks. Failure to observe these warnings may result in injury or fatality.

## 1.1.3. Maintenance

### 1.1.3.1. Components of the Side Doors

All AstroLiner T440B and T442 light rail cars have six sets of top-hung side doors. See Figure 1. Components of the side doors, on page 2. Each door set consists of a panel that slides to the right and a panel that slides to the left, operated by a pneumatic door operator.

Each set of doors has its own emergency release unit with a warning bell assembly. Each individual panel has an obstruction-detecting sensitive edge and a bottom brush seal.

**Figure 1. Components of the side doors**

### 1.1.3.2. Maintenance Schedules

Comprehensive overhaul procedures are scheduled semi-annually. Barring malfunction needing immediate attention, doors are scheduled for weekly operational checks and maintenance is performed as necessary. See Table 1. Items needing routine maintenance, on page 2. The table lists the items that should be checked each week.

**Table 1. Items needing routine maintenance**

| Item | Part number | Per car |
|---|---|---|
| Door operator | 83-48 | 4 |
| Emergency release unit | 36-95 | 2 |
| Warning bell assembly | 41-91 | 1 |
| Signal bell assembly | 78-90 | 1 |
| Brush seals | 46-94 | 8 |

### 1.1.3.3. Tools and Materials Required

Make sure that you have the following tools and materials before beginning any maintenance tasks.

- Screwdrivers

## Page 5

- Flat-head and Phillips-head
- Adjustable wrenches
- Approved lubricant—HS1200 high-speed bearing grease
- Voltage meter
- Air pressure gauge
- Approved blow dryer—Model 390 or 490

## 1.2. Procedures

### 1.2.1. Door Panel Removal

#### 1.2.1.1. When to Remove Door Panels

Remove door panels under the following conditions:

- when a door panel is physically damaged and needs to be replaced or repaired
- when a panel is jammed and approved techniques for loosening it are unsuccessful

If operations checks indicate that electrical power is not reaching the doors, or that the pneumatic system is not functioning properly, conduct additional tests on the door opera-

## Page 6

tor and repair that component as necessary.

#### 1.2.1.2. Procedure

The following procedure applies to removal of one or both door panels on a side door. As you remove the panels place all small parts on clean rags, using one rag for each type of part.

1. Unlock and lift the access panel covering the hanger assembly.

See Figure 2. Hanger assembly, on page 4. The figure shows a side view of the assembly, without the access panel.

**Figure 2. Hanger assembly**

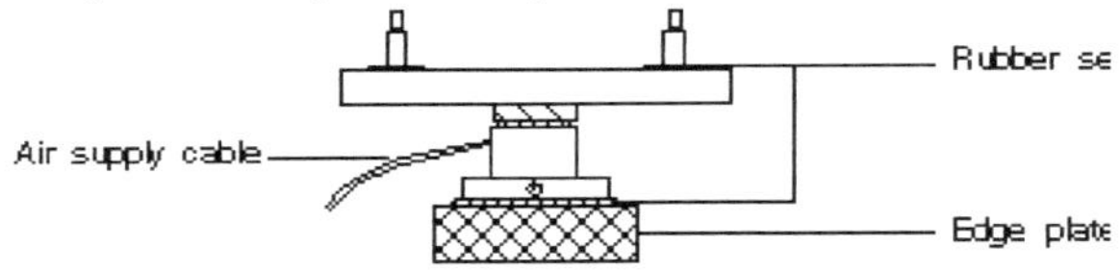

2. Unplug the air supply cable.
3. Loosen and remove the hex nuts and lock washers.
4. Remove the rubber seals.

## Structure Diagram

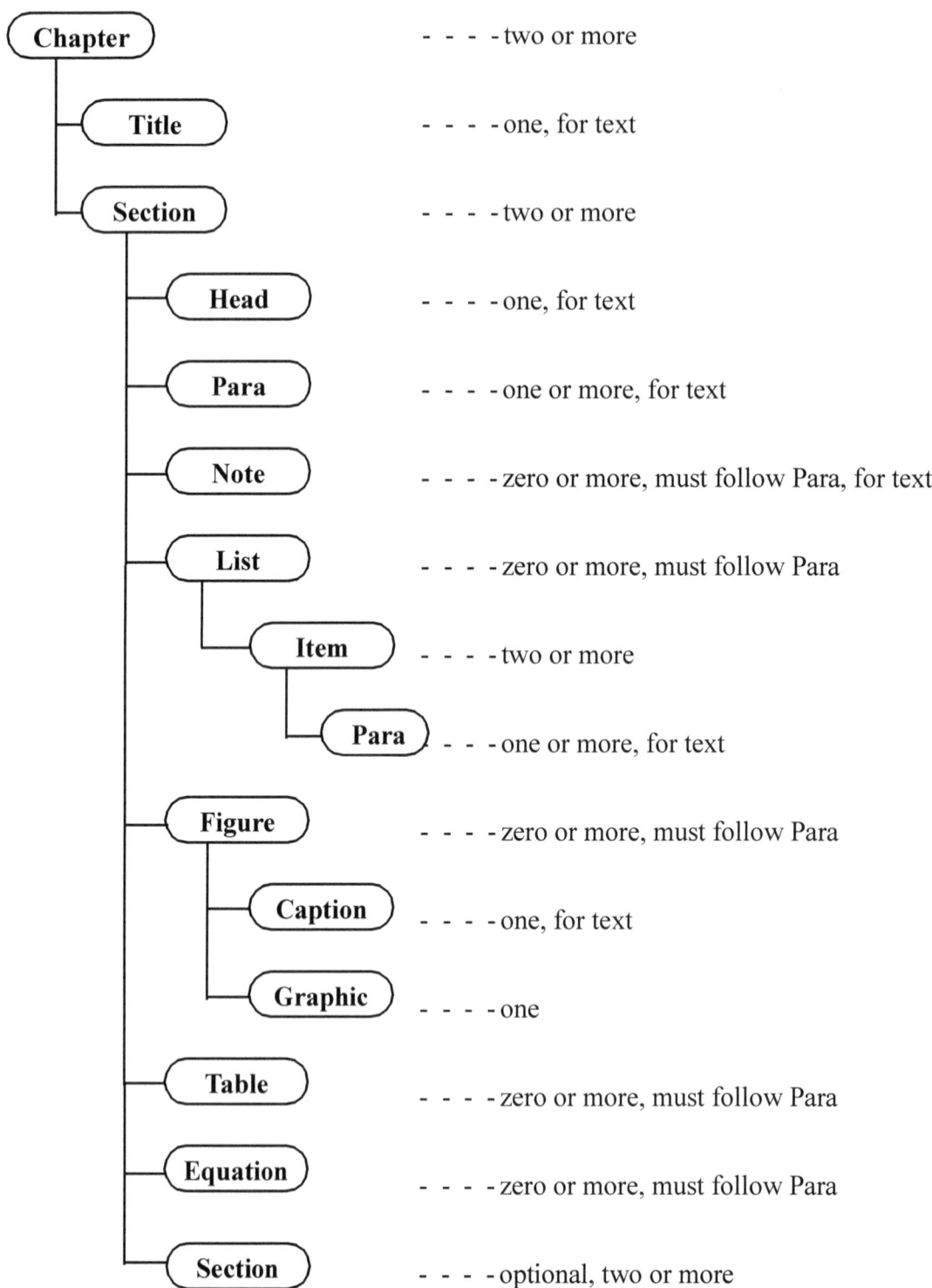

## Relationship between EDD Elements and their component parts

An EDD itself has a content model applied to it. For each type of element defined in an EDD, there are required and optional elements available. The following chart shows which objects allow or require certain other objects within their definition.

| | Comments | Tag | Type | ValidHighestLevel | GeneralRule | Inclusion & Exclusion | AutoInsertions | InitialStructurePattern | InitialTableFormat | InitialObjectFormat | SystemVariableFormatRule | AttributeList | TextFormatRules | First/LastParagraphRules | Prefix/SuffixRules |
|---|---|---|---|---|---|---|---|---|---|---|---|---|---|---|---|
| **Container** | O | R | R | R | R | O | O | | | | | O | O | O | O |
| **Table** | O | R | R | | R | O | | | O | O | | O | O | | |
| **TableTitle** | O | R | R | | R | O | | | | | | O | O | | |
| **TableHeading** | O | R | R | | R | O | O | | | | | O | O | | |
| **TableBody** | O | R | R | | R | O | O | | | | | O | O | | |
| **TableFooting** | O | R | R | | R | O | O | | | | | O | O | | |
| **TableRow** | O | R | R | | R | O | O | | | | | O | O | | |
| **TableCell** | O | R | R | | R | O | | | | | | O | O | | |
| **Footnote** | O | R | R | | R | O | | | | | | O | O | | |
| **CrossReference** | O | R | R | | | | | | | | O | O | | | |
| **Equation** | O | R | R | | | | | | | | O | O | | | |
| **Graphic** | O | R | R | | | | | | | | O | O | | | |
| **Marker** | O | R | R | | | | | | | | O | O | | | |
| **SystemVariable** | O | R | R | | | | | | | | O | O | | | |

R=Required, O=Optional

## Basic Types of Elements You Can Define

| Grouping | Type | Purpose |
|---|---|---|
| **Containers, Tables and Table Parts, Footnotes** | **Container** | General-purpose elements for text, child elements, or both |
| | **Table** | Parent of entire table |
| | **TableTitle** | Contains text for title of table |
| | **TableHeading** | Contains 1+ rows |
| | **TableBody** | Contains 1+ rows |
| | **TableFooting** | Contains 1+ rows |
| | **TableRow** | Contains 1+ cells |
| | **TableCell** | Contains text and/or child elements |
| | **Footnote** | Appears at bottom of column |
| **Objects** | **CrossReference** | For referencing other elements |
| | **Equation** | For inserting equations |
| | **Graphic** | For holding graphics |
| | **Marker** | For holding index or other markers |
| | **SystemVariable** | For inserting date, filename, or other system variables |

# Chapter 2: Initial Definition of Your First Element

## Introduction

Now that you have created and saved your EDD, you'll need to expand on the rules it will contain. The following list shows the various parts of an element definition.

Here is a list of the various things an element definition might contain:

- Comments
- Tag
- Type
- ValidHighestLevel
- GeneralRule
- Inclusion & Exclusion
- AutoInsertions
- InitialStructurePattern
- InitialTableFormat
- InitialObjectFormat
- SystemVariableFormatRule
- AttributeList
- TextFormatRules
- First/LastParagraphRules
- Prefix/SuffixRules
- Container

This module focuses on the preliminary parts: the element's **Tag**, **Comments**, **Type**, and **ValidHighestLevel** settings for your Chapter element.

You'll learn about other options for this highest level element and for other elements in subsequent chapters.

## Objectives

- Set **Elements** panel and other options to improve navigation
- Review purpose of preliminary element parts: **Tag**, **Comments**, **Type**, and **ValidHighestLevel**
- Insert the **Element** element
- Type the element **Tag**
- Insert the **Comments** and type a descriptive element comment
- Select the **Type** of element
- Specify that an element is **ValidHighestLevel** in its flow

# Setting up your editing environment

### Exercise 1: Opening your EDD

You may still have `EDD.fm` open from the previous chapter. If not, open it from your class files directory.

If you didn't complete the Chapter 1 exercises, open **Chapter 2-start Initial EDD.fm** from your class files directory and resave it as `EDD.fm`.

For instructions on downloading class files, see "Downloading class files" on page 1.

The following two exercises are optional, but will allow you to more rapidly and intuitively complete the remainder of this workbook.

### Exercise 2: Setting Toolbars

There are a number of toolbars that are shown by default in FrameMaker.

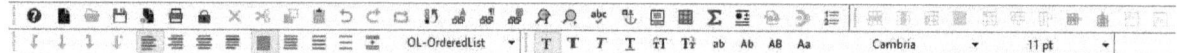

While you may find some useful, many are designed for standard unstructured FrameMaker.

In this exercise you'll hide all toolbars and then display only the Structured Access toolbar (not shown by default), which will give you quick access to many of the things you'll want to use in structured FrameMaker.

1. Navigate to **View > Toolbars > Hide All**.

   Note the reduction in clutter at the top of the screen.

2. Navigate to **View > Toolbars > Structured Access Bar**.

   The Structured Access bar appears, giving you an easy way to access the following:

   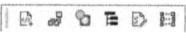

   - XML View (only active when editing XML, not SGML documents)
   - Element Catalog (brings up the **Elements** panel)
   - Edit Attributes
   - Structure View
   - Validate
   - View Element Boundaries (as tags)

You now have more room to increase the zoom of the content on your screen, and you also have less clutter to move through as you work.

Feel free to show or hide any toolbars you like, but the toolbars you just hid will not be referenced in this book.

Setting your FrameMaker environment as shown in the next 3 exercises will help you move more quickly through the material, especially if you are comfortable navigating the structure view with your cursor keys and using the Smart Insert for Elements function (Ctrl+1)

**Exercise 3: Set Elements panel options**

An EDD follows its own content model, so setting the **Elements** panel to display only the available elements will speed up your entry and will also help you understand the EDD content model itself.

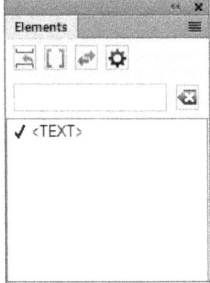

1. (if necessary) Click the **Element Catalog** button in the **Structured Access** bar to bring up the **Elements** Panel.
2. In the **Elements** panel, select the **Settings** button (⚙) to display the **Set Available Elements** dialog.
3. Select the following options:
   - Show these elements:
     Valid Elements for Working Start to Finish
   - Inclusions:
     List after Other Valid Elements
4. Select the **Set** button.

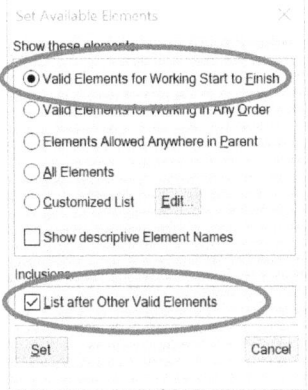

Your elements panel will now show a subset of elements, based on your current location within a document, and will show infrequently used elements (when defined as **Inclusions**) after the more frequently used elements.

> In some content models (like DITA) the **Show descriptive Element Names** option will help novice users understand the naming conventions used to label elements. The elements you'll define in this book use fairly obvious naming conventions, so enabling this option isn't critical to your success in working through the lessons.

 **Exercise 4: View Element Boundaries**

You may find that navigating within the EDD is easier when viewing the element boundaries. Viewing boundaries allows you to move more accurately within the structure view with your left and right cursor arrows.

1. Select **View > Element Boundaries** (if element boundaries are not already visible)

You should now see square brackets as shown here. If your text symbols are visible, use the **View** menu to turn off paragraph marks, or pilcrows, as they are not useful when working with structured documents and not useful in EDDs in particular.

[Automatically create formats on import.]

[[Element: ]]

Chapter 2: Initial Definition of Your First Element          Exercise 5: Set New Element Options

 **Exercise 5:  Set New Element Options**

You will significantly reduce the effort needed to insert new structure by setting behavior of new elements as shown here.

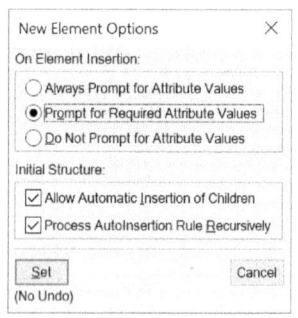

1. Navigate to **Element > New Element Options**.
2. From the **On Element Insertion:** area, select the **Prompt for Required Attribute Values** option.
3. From the **Initial Structure:** section, select the **Allow Automatic Insertion of Children** option.
4. Click the **Set** button.

## Specifying an Element Tag

An element tag is a required part of all element definitions

- An element tag is label of an element, as listed in in the **Elements** panel
- A tag may be up to 255 characters, but better to keep tags concise
- Tags are case-sensitive
- Tags can contain white space
- Characters that perform special functions in SGML or XML are not valid in Tag names. . The following characters will be used within the EDD for other functions, so an element tag cannot contain any of these special characters:

    ( ) & | , * + ? < > % [ ] = ! ; : { } "

 If you choose to mix case and use white space in element names, try to be consistent in your conventions used throughout the elements in your content model.

 **Exercise 6:  Typing the Element Tag**

In a new EDD, the first **Element** element and child **Tag** element are inserted automatically.

In this exercise, you will type the **Tag** of the first element, naming it `Chapter`.

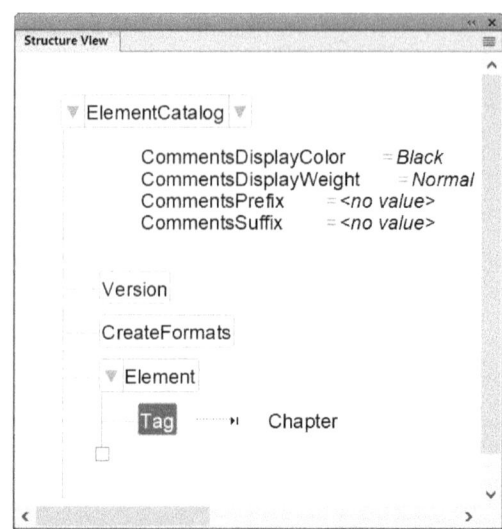

1. Open the file `EDD.fm` that you created in the previous chapter.
2. In the **Structure View** of the `EDD.fm` file, click to the right of the **Tag** element.
3. In the Tag element, type: `Chapter`
4. Save your document.

## Specifying Element Type

### Required part of all element definitions

Some elements match up to special parts, like cross-references or index markers, while many elements simply contain text or other elements. Elements containing text or other elements are generally defined as **Containers**.

  **Exercise 7: Identifying the Element as a Container**

In this exercise, you will identify **Chapter** as a **Container** element. To do this, click below the **Tag** element, in the **Chapter** element definition.

1. In the **Structure View**, click below the **Tag** element, above the red square beneath the **Element** element.

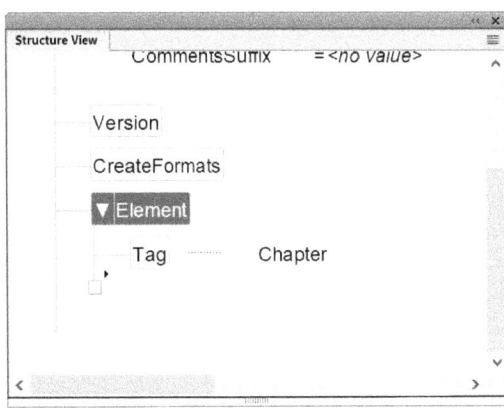

 When positioning the cursor in the structure view, practice clicking where the triangle will appear. You'll be less likely to improperly position the cursor if you can predict (and click on) the area where the triangle will display.

2. From the **Elements** panel, insert a **Container** element.

    The **Container** element and **GeneralRule** child elements appear automatically.

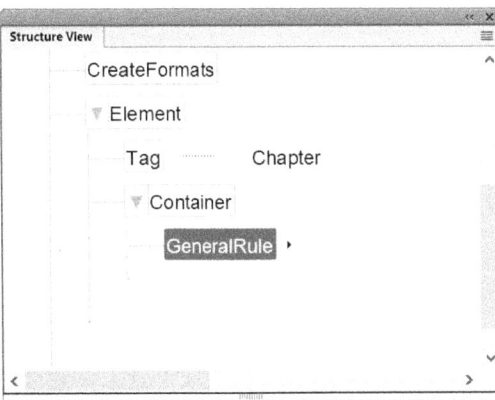

 If the **General Rule** element doesn't appear automatically, set **Element > New Element Options** to **Allow Automatic Insertion of Children**.

You'll learn about and define the **GeneralRule** in the next chapter.

3. Save your changes.

## Specifying a ValidHighestLevel Element

### A required part of at least one container element definition for each structured flow

- Identifies a container that will hold all elements in flow
- Also required for the highest-level element for book files
- The **ValidHighestLevel** element can appear above or below general rule

### Exercise 8:   Specifying an element as ValidHighestLevel

In this exercise, you will insert a **ValidHighestLevel** element to define the **Chapter** element as valid at the highest level in its structured flow. A **ValidHighestLevel** element may be placed either above or below a **GeneralRule** element.

1. In the **Structure View**, click above or below the **GeneralRule** element, on the line descending from the **Container** element.

The screen capture below shows the **ValidHighestLevel** placed **above** the **GeneralRule** element.

2. From the **Elements** panel, insert a **ValidHighestLevel** element.

   A **ValidHighestLevel** element and **Yes** child element appear.

3. Save your changes.

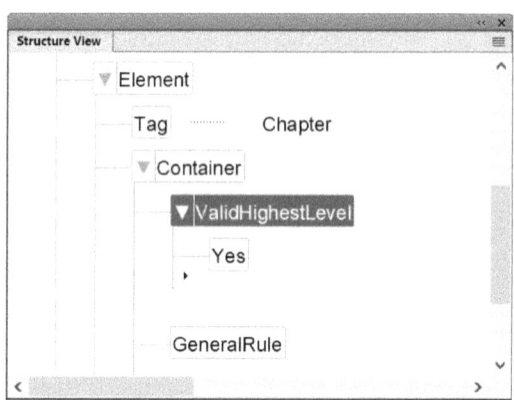

## Placing Comments in Element Definitions

### An optional part of all element definitions

- Allows you to type a description of an element in your own words
- Comments may contain an unlimited number of characters
- Must be placed above the **Tag** element

Chapter 2: Initial Definition of Your First Element    Exercise 9: Commenting the Element Definition

 **Exercise 9: Commenting the Element Definition**

In this exercise, you will insert a **Comments** element and add a comment describing your **Chapter** element.

1. In the **Structure View**, click above the **Tag** element, on the line descending from **Element** element.

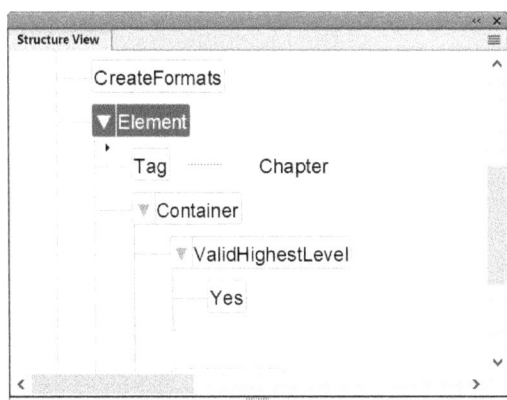

2. Double-click on the **Comments** element in the **Elements** panel.

   A **Comments** element appears.

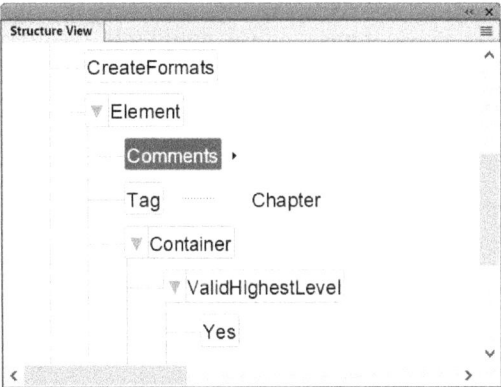

3. In the **Comments** element, type:

   ```
   Chapter is the container for all elements within chapters of
   maintenance manuals
   ```

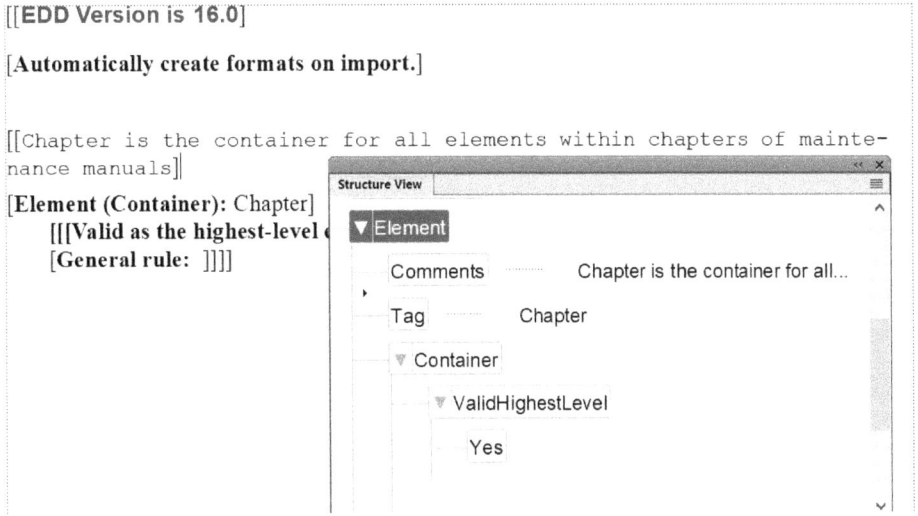

23

4. Collapse the element to see that the comment snippet shows now instead of the tag name.

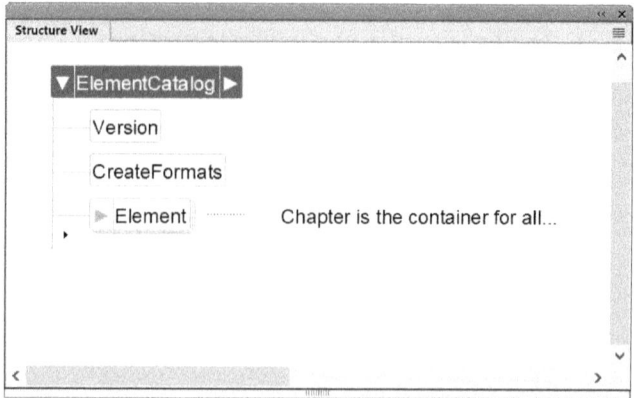

 Prefacing the comment with the tag name is a good idea, since when collapsed, only the first few characters of the comment (the snippet) display, instead of the tag name.

## Moving forward

Your new EDD has an element, but now needs much more before you can start to use it. In the next chapter you'll define basic chapter components and see how your element definitions will evolve as you add necessary structure options.

# Chapter 3: GeneralRule for Containers and Footnotes

## Introduction

This chapter focuses on defining the **GeneralRule** for **Container** elements and **Footnote** elements.

### Objectives

- Create a **GeneralRule** for **Container** elements and **Footnote** elements
- Learn about occurrence indicators and connectors in a **GeneralRule**
- Use content symbols and parentheses in a **GeneralRule**
- Review the default **GeneralRule** for **Container** and **Footnote** elements
- Import your EDD into the structured template
- Test your element definitions in the structured template

### Overview

General rules are a required part of element definitions for:

- Containers
- Table, TableTitle, TableHeading, TableBody, TableFooting, TableRow, TableCell elements
- Footnotes

General rules specify:

- The child elements allowable in an element
- Whether child elements are required or optional
- The frequency in which child elements can occur
- The order in which child elements can occur
- Whether element may contain <TEXT>

 Elements defined in your EDD must be referenced in at least one general rule.
Elements referenced in a general rule must be defined in your EDD.

25

## Syntax

Refer to this page as needed to complete the exercises in this chapter.

### Connectors

You can use connectors to separate multiple element tags in **GeneralRule** and to specify order of child elements

Here are the connectors allowable in a general rule:

| Symbol | Meaning | Example |
|---|---|---|
| Comma (,) | Elements are mandatory and must occur in the specified order | TableTitle, TableHead, TableBody |
| Ampersand (&) | Elements are mandatory, but can occur in any order | Caption & Graphic |
| Vertical bar (\|) | Any one element in the group can occur | Warning \| Note \| Caution |

### Occurence Indicators

Occurrence indicators allow you to specify whether a child is required or optional, and if it can be repeated

Here are the occurrence indicators allowable in a general rule:

| Symbol | Meaning | Alternate Description |
|---|---|---|
| No indicator | Child is required and must occur only once | Requires 1 |
| Question mark (?) | Child is optional and can occur once | May occur 0 or 1 time |
| Asterisk (*) | Child is optional and can occur more than once | May occur 0 or more times |
| Plus sign (+) | Child is required and can occur more than once | Must occur 1 or more times |

### Special Content Types

You can use content strings to specify content other than child elements and to indicate elements with no content

| String | Meaning |
|---|---|
| <TEXT> | Can contain text and any inclusions |
| <TEXTONLY> | Can contain only text<br>Cannot contain child elements, even inclusions defined in ancestors' content rules |
| <ANY> | Can contain any combination of text and elements defined in EDD |
| <EMPTY> | Cannot contain any text or elements |

## Writing the initial GeneralRules for basic elements

### Exercise 1: Writing a GeneralRule for a Chapter element

In this exercise, you will define the **GeneralRule** for the **Chapter** element's contents, as one **Title** element, following by two or more **Section** elements.

1. If it is not already open, open `EDD.fm`, from the directory containing your class files.

   If you didn't complete the previous chapter exercises, open up the
   **Chapter 3-start Containers.fm** file in your class directory and save it as `EDD.fm` in your class files directory.

For instructions on downloading class files, see "Downloading class files" on page 1.

2. In the **Structure View**, click to the right of the **GeneralRule** element.

3. In the GeneralRule element, type:
   **Title, Section, Section+**

   Commas specify an explicit order. Spaces aren't essential but are helpful for readability.

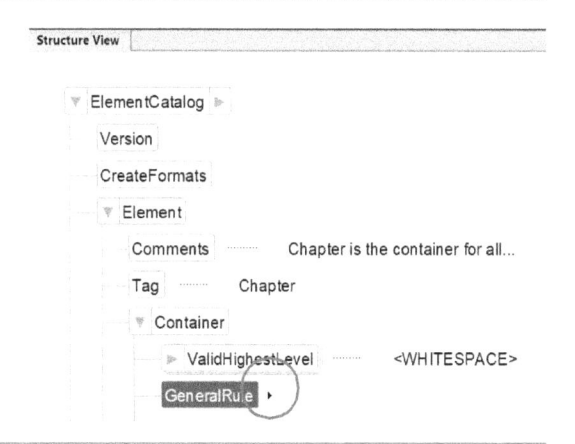

You might interpret this rule as "A valid chapter must contain a title, followed by a section, followed by one or more optional sections" or "A valid chapter must contain a title, followed by two or more sections."

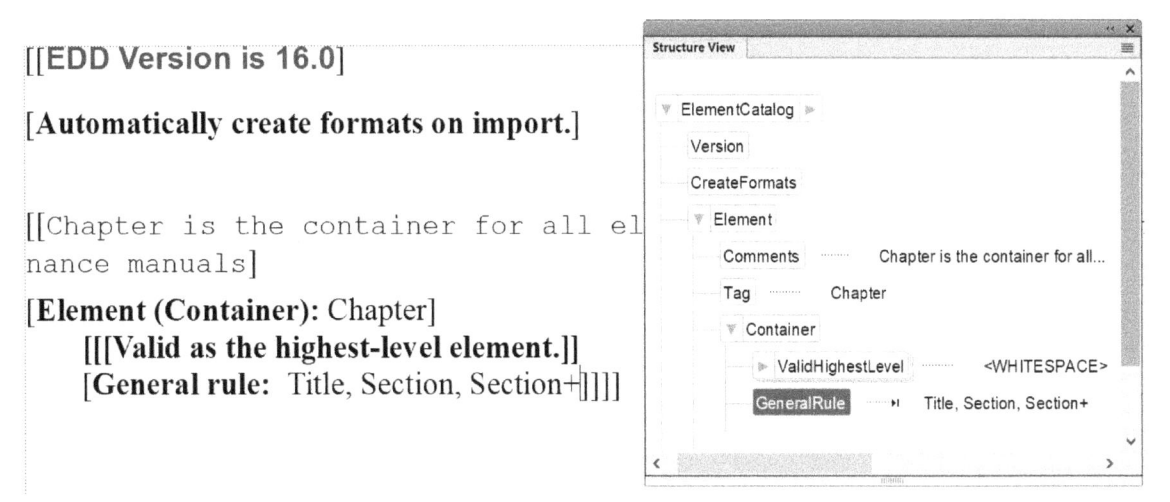

[[EDD Version is 16.0]

[Automatically create formats on import.]

[[Chapter is the container for all el
nance manuals]
[Element (Container): Chapter
    [[[Valid as the highest-level element.]]
    [General rule: Title, Section, Section+]]]]

4. Save your changes.

27

> Elements referenced in a General Rule must be defined. Elements defined in the EDD must be referenced in a General Rule, unless they are Valid at Highest Level

Now that you have referenced a **Title** and a **Section** in a **GeneralRule**, you will need to define these elements.

### Exercise 2: Defining a Title element

In this exercise you will create a new container element called **Title** with a **GeneralRule** of **<TEXT>**.

To add your title element, do the following:

1. In the **Structure View**, click at the end of your EDD, below **Element** for the **Chapter** tag, on the line descending from the **ElementCatalog** element.

2. From the **Elements** panel, insert an **Element** element.

   The **Element** and child **Tag** element appear.

3. With the insertion point to the right of the **Tag** element, type: `Title`

4. Click below the **Tag** element, above the red square beneath the **Element** element.

5. From the **Elements** panel, insert **Container**.

   The **Container** element and **GeneralRule** child element appear.

6. With the insertion point to the right of the **GeneralRule** element, type: **<TEXT>**

7. Save your changes.

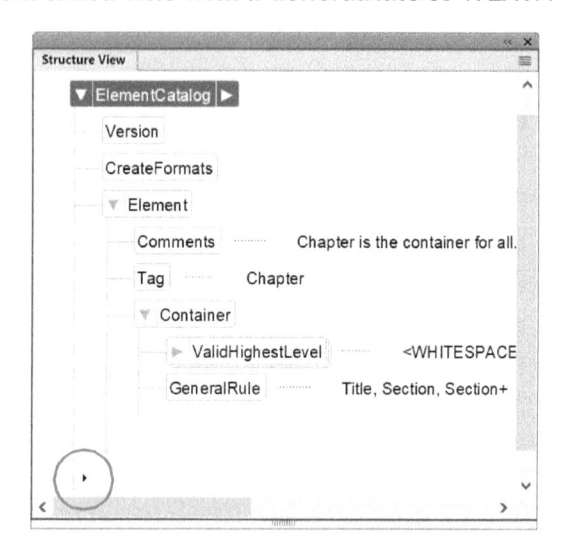

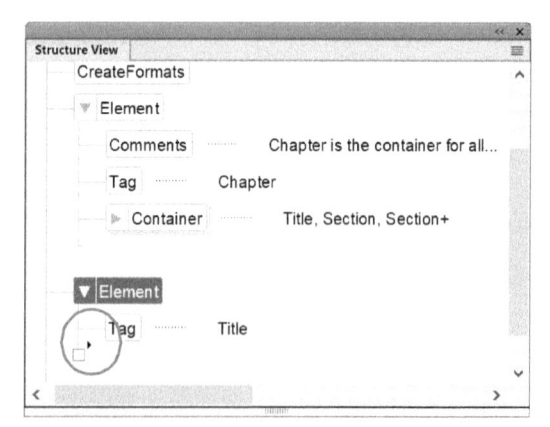

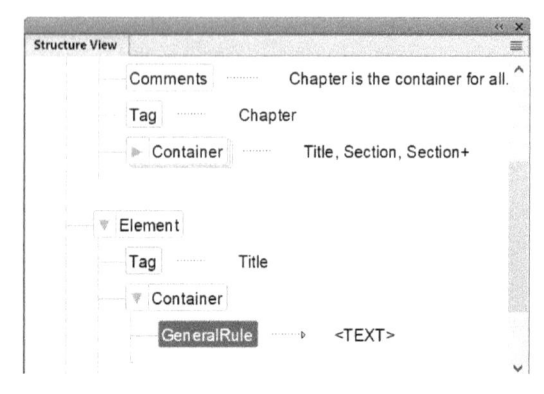

> At this point you may want to start collapsing elements in your **Structure View** to improve navigation.

### Exercise 3: Defining Section, a container of child elements

In this exercise, you will define the **Section** element that will (for now) require a **Head** element followed by one or more **Para** elements. The GeneralRule for the **Section** element will be one of the most frequently modified elements in this course.

To define your section element, do the following:

1. In the **Structure View**, click below the **Title** element definition, on the line descending from the **ElementCatalog** element.

2. Insert **Element** from the **Elements** panel.

   The **Element** and its child, **Tag** appear.
   (not shown in screen capture)

3. With the insertion point to the right of the **Tag** element, type: `Section`

4. Click below the **Tag** element, above the red square at the end of the **Element** element.

5. From the **Elements** panel, insert a **Container** element.

   **Container** and its child, **GeneralRule** appear. (not shown in screen capture)

6. With the insertion point to the right of the **GeneralRule** element, type: `Head, Para+`

   The **+** indicates that Para is required, and can occur more than once.

7. Save your changes.

Next, you'll define these two newly specified elements.

> White space is ignored when working with connectors. This means you are free to add white space in and around connectors to make the EDD more easily readable.

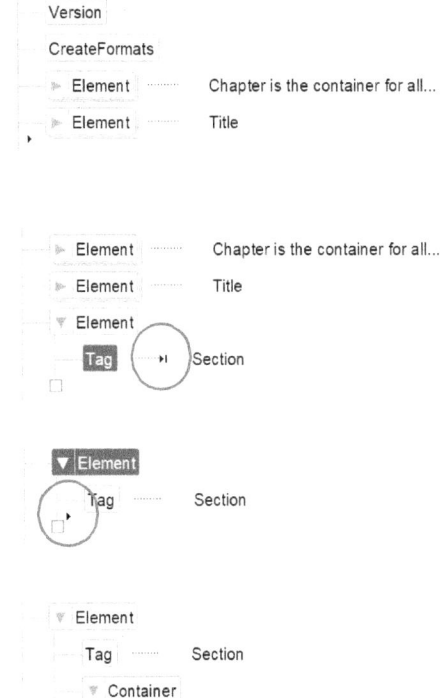

## Exercise 4: Defining More Descendant Container Elements

In this exercise, you will define the **Head** and **Para** elements referenced in the previous exercise. If you like, you can match the screen captures shown for each element.

To insert your new elements, do the following:

1. Create a new **Element** as a sibling to **Section** and tag it **Head**.
   a. In the **Structure View**, click below the definition for the **Section** tag, on the line descending from the **ElementCatalog** element.
   b. From the **Elements** panel, insert an **Element** element.
   
   The **Element** and child **Tag** element appear.
   
   c. In the **Tag** element, type: `Head`

2. Define **Head** as a **Container** with a **GeneralRule** of `<TEXT>`
   a. Click below the **Tag** element.
   b. From the **Elements** panel, insert **Container**.
   
   The **Container** element and **GeneralRule** child element appear.
   
   c. In the **GeneralRule** element, type: `<TEXT>`

3. Create a new **Element** and tag it `Para`.
   a. In the **Structure View**, click below the last **Element** element.
   b. From the **Elements** panel, insert an **Element** element.
   
   The **Element** and child **Tag** element appear.
   
   c. In the **Tag** element, type: `Para`

4. Define **Para** as a **Container** with a **GeneralRule** of `<TEXT>`
   a. Click below the **Tag** element.
   b. From the **Elements** panel, insert **Container**.
   
   **Container** element and **GeneralRule** child element appear.
   
   c. In the **GeneralRule** element, type: `<TEXT>`

5. Save your changes.

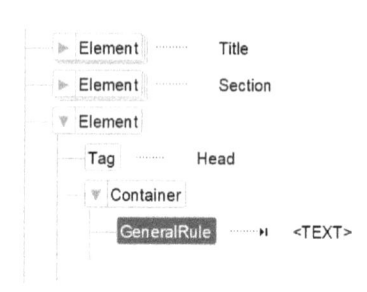

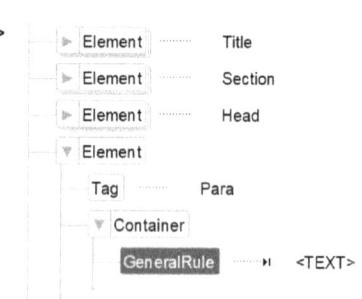

## Importing and Testing

### Exercise 5: Importing the EDD

In this exercise, you will create a new portrait document, save it as your structured template, then import the element definitions defined in the EDD into your structured template.

1. Create a new portrait document.
   a. Select **File > New > Document**.
      The **New** dialog box appears.
   b. Click **Portrait**.
      A new blank document appears.
2. Use the **Save As** dialog box to save the new portrait document in your class files directory with the new filename `testdoc.fm`.
   a. From the **File** menu, choose **Save As**.
      The **Save Document** dialog box appears.
   b. If necessary, change to your class files directory.
   c. In the **Save in File** field, delete the current file name and type: `testdoc.fm`
   d. Click **Save**.
3. Ensure that your cursor is in the text flow and then look at the **Elements** panel.
   This is currently an unstructured document and the **Elements** panel is empty because there are no elements available for you to insert.
4. Ensure that `testdoc.fm` is the active file and choose **File > Import > Element Definitions**.
   The **Import Element Definitions** dialog box appears.
5. From the **Import from Document** dropdown menu, choose `EDD.fm`.

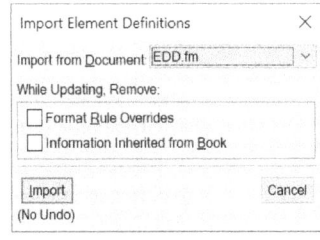

> ⚠️ If the EDD isn't open in FrameMaker, it will not appear in the menu as a choice for import.

6. Click **Import**.
   An alert appears indicating completion of the import process.
7. Click **OK** to close the alert box.
8. If errors exist in the element definitions, a log file will appear identifying the problems.
   If this occurs, edit your EDD to correct the errors and repeat steps 3 through 6.

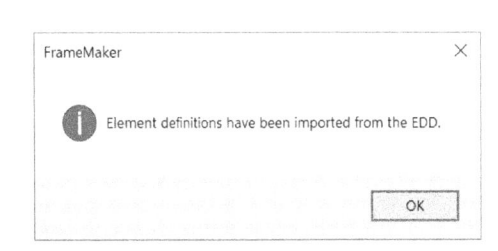

If no errors appear, FrameMaker has successfully added and/or updated the element definitions in the element catalog of `testdoc.fm`.

9. Save your changes.

## Exercise 6: Testing the EDD

In this exercise, you will test your **Chapter**, **Title**, **Section**, **Head**, and **Para** element definitions by inserting elements and typing text into elements defined to contain text.

1. Choose **View > Element Boundaries**.

   This will display the square brackets around content once you've added elements to your document.

2. If not already visible, show the **Elements** and **Structure View** panels.

3. Set available elements to **Valid Elements for Working Start to Finish**.

   a. Choose **Element > Set Available Elements**.

   The **Set Available Elements** dialog box appears.

   b. In **Show Tags For**, turn on **Valid Elements for Working Start to Finish**.

   c. In **Inclusions**, choose **List after Other Valid Elements**.

   d. Click **Set**.

   The **Elements** panel displays only the **Chapter** element as the element valid at the highest level in the structure.

   If you don't see **Chapter** in the **Elements** panel, place your cursor inside of the text frame in the Document Window.

4. From the **Elements** panel, insert a **Chapter** element.

   The **Structure View** displays the **Chapter** element bubble, the **Document Window** displays element boundaries for the **Chapter** element, and the **Elements** panel displays an available **Title** child element.

5. Insert a **Title** element.

   The **Elements** panel displays **<TEXT>**, indicating that you can type in this element.

6. In the **Title** element, type:
   ```
   Title of Chapter in Maintenance
   Manual
   ```

   (screen capture not shown)

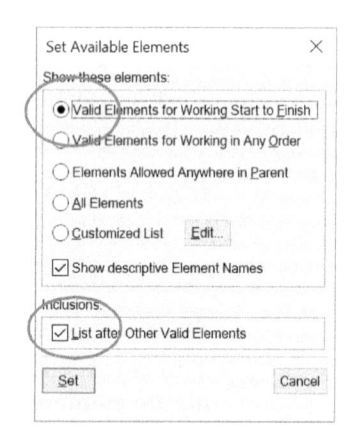

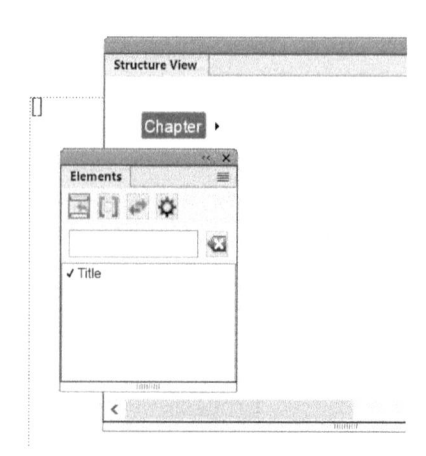

7. Click below the **Title** element and insert a **Section** element.

   The **Elements** panel updates to reflect the new position of your cursor within the document.

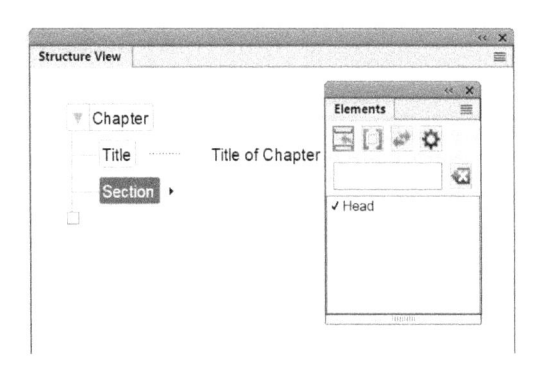

8. Insert a **Head** element and type:
   `Heading for First Section`

9. Click below the **Head** element, insert a **Para** element, and type: `Text for first paragraph within Section.`

10. Click below the **Para** element and insert several more **Para** elements to verify that you can insert more than one **Para** element. (screen capture not shown)

    Notice the red square on the line descending from the **Chapter** element.

    That's because **Chapter** is required to have two or more **Section** elements.

11. Insert another **Section** element, a **Head**, and at least two **Para** elements.

    Don't bother to type any more text. You are just testing, and you have already made sure that you can type in these elements when you inserted them in the first Section.

    Notice how the red square disappears once the **Section** requirement is satisfied.

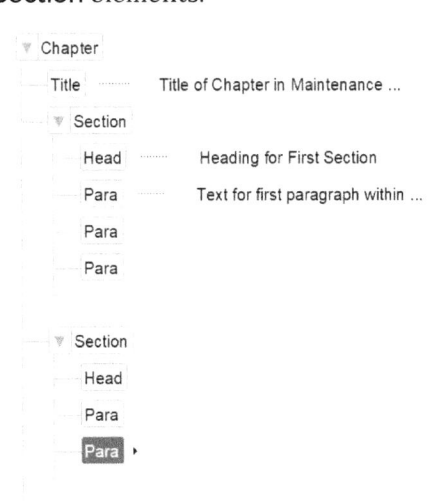

Chapter 3: GeneralRule for Containers and Footnotes        Adding to, modifying, and updating the EDD

12. You may recall that the **GeneralRule** for **Chapter** allows for two *or more* **Section** elements.

    Insert a third **Section** element to verify that you can insert more than two consecutive **Section** elements.

13. Save your changes.

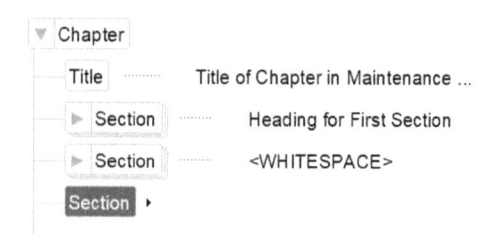

## Adding to, modifying, and updating the EDD

✓ From this point on, exercises will include changes to **GeneralRule** content in the EDD. The additional text for these definitions are marked in bold.

### Exercise 7: Expanding the Section GeneralRule

In this exercise, you will redefine the **Section** element's **GeneralRule** to allow an optional **WarnNote** element that will contain <TEXT>. Then you will define the newly referenced **WarnNote** element.

Modify your **Section** general rule as follows:

1. In the EDD, locate the element definition for the **Section** element.
2. In the **Document Window**, change the **GeneralRule** as follows:

   `Head, (Para, WarnNote?)+`

   The newly referenced **WarnNote** element requires a definition.

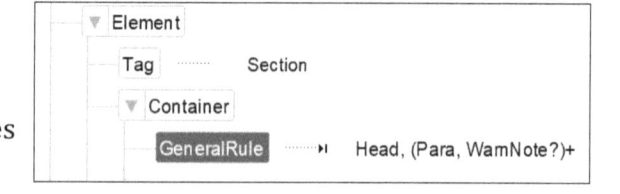

3. Create a new **Element** and tag it **WarnNote**.
   a. In the **Structure View**, click below the last **Element** element.
   b. From the **Elements** panel, insert an **Element** element.

      An **Element** and a child **Tag** element appear.

   c. In the **Tag** element, type: `WarnNote`

4. Define **WarnNote** as a **Container** with a **GeneralRule** of <TEXT>
   a. Click below the **Tag** element.
   b. From the **Elements** panel, insert **Container**.

      **Container** element and **GeneralRule** child element appear.

   c. In the **GeneralRule** element, type: `<TEXT>`

✓ You can use Copy/Paste to speed creation of similar structure.

5. Save your changes.

34

## Exercise 8: Referencing a Group Within a Group

In this exercise, you will redefine **Section** to allow for more complex combinations of elements.

To modify the Section general rule, do the following:

1. In the EDD, locate the element definition for the **Section** element.
2. In the **Document Window**, change the **GeneralRule** as follows:
   ```
   Head, (Para, (WarnNote | List)?)+
   ```
3. Create a new **Element** and tag it **List**.
   a. In the **Structure View**, click below the last **Element** element.
   b. From the **Elements** panel, insert an **Element** element.
      The **Element** and child **Tag** element appear.
   c. In the **Tag** element, type: `List`
4. Define **List** as a **Container** with a **GeneralRule** of Item, Item+
   a. Click below the **Tag** element.
   b. From the **Elements** panel, insert **Container**.
      A **Container** element and **GeneralRule** child element appear.
   c. In the **GeneralRule** element, type: `Item, Item+`
5. Create a new **Element** and tag it **Item**.
   a. In the **Structure View**, click below the last **Element** element.
   b. From the **Elements** panel, insert an **Element** element.
      The **Element** and child **Tag** element appear.
   c. In the Tag element, type: `Item`
6. Define **Item** as a **Container** with a **GeneralRule** of <TEXT>
   a. Click below the **Tag** element.
   b. From the **Elements** panel, insert **Container**.
      **Container** and child **GeneralRule** elements appear.
   c. In the **GeneralRule** element, type: `<TEXT>`
7. Save your changes.

## Exercise 9: Reimporting and Retesting

In this exercise, you will reimport the EDD into the structured template and test your element definitions for **Section**, **WarnNote**, **List**, and **Item**.

1. Reimport your element definitions and fix any errors.
   a. In `testdoc.fm`, from the **File** menu, choose **Import > Element Definitions**.
      The **Import Element Definitions** dialog appears.
   b. From the **Import from Document** dropdown menu, choose `EDD.fm`.

c. Click **Import**.

An alert box appears indicating "**Element definitions have been imported from the EDD**"

d. Click **OK** to close the alert box.

> ⚠ If you had errors in the element definitions, edit your EDD and reimport.

> ✓ If you did not have errors, a log file will not appear and you do not need to edit your EDD and reimport before testing.

FrameMaker replaces element definitions in the **Elements** panel of the structured template.

2. In the **Structure View**, click on the line descending from any **Section** element but below a **Para** element.

3. From the **Elements** panel, insert a **WarnNote** element and type any text to test it.

4. Click on the line descending from any **Section** element but below a **Para** element.

5. Insert a **List** element.

6. In the **List** element, insert an **Item** element and type any text to test it.

7. Notice the red square on the line descending from the **List** element.

   A **List** must have two or more **Item** elements to conform to the content model.

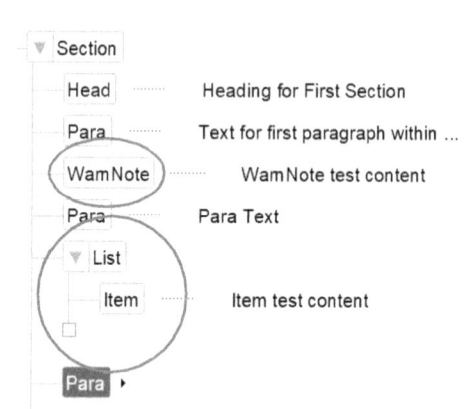

8. Insert several more **Item** elements to verify that you can have as many as needed.

9. Try inserting two consecutive **WarnNote** elements.

   Upon insertion of the second element a red square appears between the elements. This indicates that other content (in this case, a Para) is needed between two consecutive **WarnNote** elements.

10. Try inserting two consecutive **List** elements.

    Upon insertion of the second element a red square appears between the elements. This indicates that other content (in this case, a Para) is needed between two consecutive **List** elements.

11. Try inserting a **List** immediately after a **WarnNote**, or vice versa.

    Upon insertion of the second element a red square appears between the elements. This indicates that other content (in this case, a Para) is needed between **List** and **WarnNote** elements.

12. Try inserting a **List** after a **Head**.

    Upon insertion of the second element a red square appears between the elements. This indicates that other content (in this case, a Para) is needed between **Head** and **List** elements.

13. Save your changes.

## Exercise 10: Referencing an Element Within Itself

In this exercise, you will redefine the **Section** element's **GeneralRule** to allow nested sections.

To do this:

1. In the EDD, locate the element definition for the **Section** element.
2. In the Document Window, change the **GeneralRule** as follows:

    ```
    Head, (Para, (WarnNote | List)?)+, (Section, Section+)?
    ```

3. Save your changes.
4. Reimport your element definitions and fix any errors.

    a. In `testdoc.fm`, from the **File** menu, choose **Import > Element Definitions**.

    The **Import Element Definitions** dialog appears.

    b. From the **Import from Document** dropdown menu, choose `EDD.fm`.

    c. Click **Import**.

    An alert box appears indicating "**Element definitions have been imported from the EDD**"

    d. Click **OK** to close the alert box.

> If you had errors in the element definitions, edit your EDD and reimport.

5. Practice inserting **Section** elements.

    Recognize that whenever you insert a **Section** element, you must insert two or more at the same level, and they must be the last two children of their parent.

6. Save your changes.

## Exercise 11: Referencing and Defining a Footnote Element

In this exercise, you will redefine the **Para** element's **GeneralRule** to allow both text and footnote elements. Then, you will define a **Footnote** element that takes advantage of FrameMaker's existing footnote functionality.

To allow for footnotes, do the following:

1. In the EDD, locate the element definition for the **Para** element.
2. In the Document Window, change the **GeneralRule** as follows:

    ```
    (<TEXT> | Footnote)+
    ```

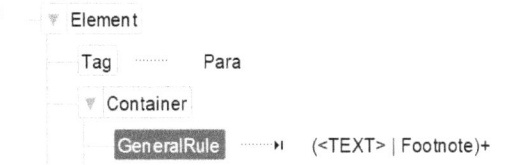

3. Insert a new **Element** and tag it **Footnote**.

    a. In the **Structure View**, click below the last **Element** element.

    b. From the **Elements** panel, insert an **Element** element.

    An **Element** and a child **Tag** element appear.

    c. In the **Tag** element, type: `Footnote`

4. Define **Footnote** as a **Footnote** with a **GeneralRule** of <TEXT>
   a. Click below the **Tag** element.
   b. From the **Elements** panel, insert **Footnote**.
      **Footnote** element and **GeneralRule** child element appear.
   c. In the **GeneralRule** element, type: `<TEXT>`
5. Save your changes.
6. Reimport your element definitions into your test document. If you had errors when importing the element definitions, correct your EDD and reimport.
7. Confirm that the changes you made to the EDD are working as expected.
8. In the **Structure View**, click on the line descending from any **Section** element.
9. From the **Elements** panel, insert a **Para** element and type any text to test it.
10. With your insertion point still in the text, insert a **Footnote** element and type any text to test it.
11. Click below the Footnote element, on the line descending from the Para element, and type a little more text.
12. With your insertion point still in the text, insert another **Footnote** element and type any text to verify that you can insert multiple **Footnote** elements in a **Para** element.
13. Try inserting a **Footnote** element in a **Head** element.

    You cannot. In your EDD, **General Rules** are currently written so that **Footnote** elements can be children of **Para** elements, not **Head** or other elements.
14. Save your changes.

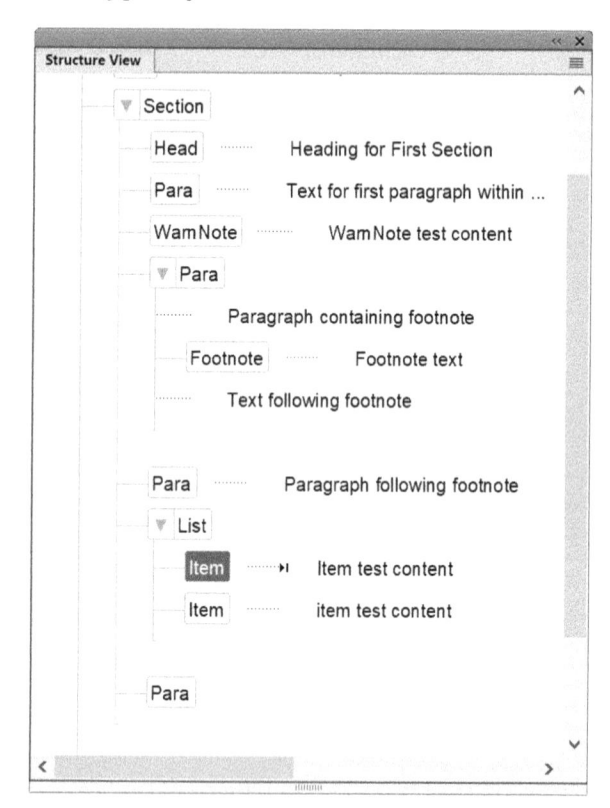

# Chapter 4: GeneralRule for Tables and Table Parts

## Introduction

This chapter focuses on defining the **GeneralRule** for **Table** elements and table part elements.

### Objectives

- Write **GeneralRule** for **Table** element
- Write **GeneralRule** for table part elements—**TableTitle, TableHeading, TableBody, TableFooting, TableRow, TableCell**
- Review default **GeneralRules**
- Review restrictions on **GeneralRules** for **Table** and table part elements
- Reimport the EDD into the structured template
- Test **Table** and table part element definitions in the structured template

### Overview

General rules are a required part of element definitions for:

- Containers
- Table, TableTitle, TableHeading, TableBody, TableFooting, TableRow, TableCell elements
- Footnotes

General rules specify:

- The child elements allowable in an element
- Whether child elements are required or optional
- The frequency in which child elements can occur
- The order in which child elements can occur
- Whether element may contain <TEXT>

> ⚠ Elements defined in your EDD must be referenced in at least one general rule.
> Elements referenced in a general rule must be defined in your EDD.

## Syntax

Refer to this page as needed to complete the exercises in this chapter.

### Connectors

You can use connectors to separate multiple element tags in **GeneralRule** and to specify order of child elements

Here are the connectors allowable in a general rule:

| Symbol | Meaning | Example |
|---|---|---|
| Comma (,) | Elements are mandatory and must occur in the specified order | TableTitle, TableHead, TableBody |
| Ampersand (&) | Elements are mandatory, but can occur in any order | Caption & Graphic |
| Vertical bar (\|) | Any one element in the group can occur | Warning \| Note \| Caution |

### Occurence Indicators

Occurrence indicators allow you to specify whether a child is required or optional, and if it can be repeated

Here are the occurrence indicators allowable in a general rule:

| Symbol | Meaning | Alternate Description |
|---|---|---|
| No indicator | Child is required and must occur only once | Requires 1 |
| Question mark (?) | Child is optional and can occur once | May occur 0 or 1 time |
| Asterisk (*) | Child is optional and can occur more than once | May occur 0 or more times |
| Plus sign (+) | Child is required and can occur more than once | Must occur 1 or more times |

### Special Content Types

You can use content strings to specify content other than child elements and to indicate elements with no content

| String | Meaning |
|---|---|
| <TEXT> | Can contain text and any inclusions |
| <TEXTONLY> | Can contain only text<br>Cannot contain child elements, even inclusions defined in ancestors' content rules |
| <ANY> | Can contain any combination of text and elements defined in EDD |
| <EMPTY> | Cannot contain any text or elements |

## GeneralRule Restrictions

| Element type | Restrictions |
|---|---|
| **Table** | • Limited to one each of TableTitle, TableHeading, TableBody, TableFooting (in that order)<br>• TableBody is required<br>• TableTitle, TableHeading, TableFooting are optional<br>• No plus sign (+), asterisk (*), ampersand (&)<br>• No <TEXT>, <TEXTONLY>, <ANY>, <EMPTY> |
| **TableTitle** | • All child elements are allowed, except Table and table parts<br>• <TEXT>, <TEXTONLY>, <ANY>, <EMPTY> allowed |
| **TableHeading** | • One or more TableRow child elements<br>• No <TEXT>, <TEXTONLY>, <ANY>, <EMPTY> |
| **TableBody** | • One or more TableRow child elements<br>• No <TEXT>, <TEXTONLY>, <ANY>, <EMPTY> |
| **TableFooting** | • One or more TableRow child elements<br>• No <TEXT>, <TEXTONLY>, <ANY>, <EMPTY> |
| **TableRow** | • One or more TableCell child elements<br>• No <TEXT>, <TEXTONLY>, <ANY>, <EMPTY> |
| **TableCell** | • All child elements are allowed, except Table and table parts<br>• <TEXT>, <TEXTONLY>, <ANY>, <EMPTY> allowed |

## Default GeneralRule

If you import an EDD with an empty GeneralRule element into a document, FrameMaker inserts a default GeneralRule. Here are the default general rules for table parts:

| Element Type | Default GeneralRule |
|---|---|
| Table | TITLE?, HEADING?, BODY, FOOTING? |
| TableTitle | <ANY> |
| TableHeading | ROW+ |
| TableBody | ROW+ |
| TableFooting | ROW+ |
| TableRow | CELL+ |
| TableCell | <ANY> |

# Referencing and Defining the Table Element

**Exercise 1: Referencing a Table Element in a GeneralRule**

In this exercise, you will redefine the **Section** element's **GeneralRule** to contain optional **Table** elements.

1. If it is not already open, from your class files directory, open `EDD.fm`, the EDD you've been modifying throughout the class.

   If you did not finish the previous chapter's modifications to the EDD, please open **Chapter 4-start Tables.fm** instead, and save it in your class files directory as `EDD.fm`.

   For instructions on downloading class files, see "Downloading class files" on page 1.

2. In the EDD, locate the element definition for the **Section** element.
3. In the **Document Window**, change the **GeneralRule** as follows:

   ```
   Head, (Para, (WarnNote | List | Table)?)+, (Section, Section+)?
   ```

   > [[**Element (Container):** Section]
   >     [[**General rule:** Head, (Para, (WarnNote | List | Table)?)+, (Section, Section+)?]]]

4. Save your changes.

**Exercise 2: Defining a Table Element**

In this exercise, you will define the **Table** element. At a minimum, FrameMaker requires that a table have a body of one row with one cell, but you will put tighter restrictions on your table by creating a general rule requiring a **TableTitle** and a **TableHeading**

In subsequent exercises, you will put even tighter restrictions on your table.

To define the **Table** element:

1. Add an element definition to the EDD and tag it **Table**.
   a. In the **Structure View**, click below the last **Element**.
   b. From the **Elements** panel, insert an **Element**.
      An **Element** and **Tag** child element appear.
   c. In the **Tag** element, type: `Table`
2. Define **Table** as a **Table** with a **GeneralRule** of TableTitle, TableHeading, TableBody, TableFooting?
   a. Click below the **Tag** element.
   b. From the **Elements** panel, insert **Table**.
   c. A **Table** element and **GeneralRule** child element appear.

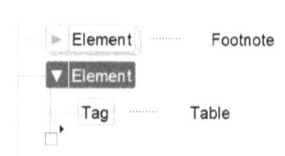

d. In **GeneralRule** element, type:
```
TableTitle, TableHeading, TableBody, TableFooting?
```

> [[**Element (Table):** Table]¶
>     [[**General rule:**〉TableTitle, TableHeading, TableBody, TableFooting?]]]]§

3. Save your changes.

Next you will define the new table parts you referenced in this rule.

# Defining Table Part Elements

### Exercise 3: Defining a TableTitle Element

To define the **TableTitle** element:

1. Add an element definition to the EDD and tag it **TableTitle**.
   a. In the **Structure View**, click below the last **Element**.
   b. From the **Elements** panel, insert an **Element**.
      An **Element** and a **Tag** child element appear.
   c. In the Tag element, type: `TableTitle`

2. Define **TableTitle** as a **TableTitle** with a **GeneralRule** of `<TEXT>`
   a. Click below the **Tag** element.
   b. From the **Elements** panel, insert **TableTitle**.
      A **TableTitle** element and a **GeneralRule** child element appear.
   c. In the **GeneralRule** element, type: `<TEXT>`

3. Save your changes.

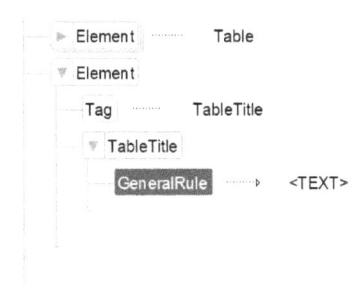

### Exercise 4: Defining a TableHeading Element

In this exercise, you will define the **TableHeading** element, by:

- Inserting an **Element** and typing the **Tag** as **TableHeading**
- Inserting a **TableHeading** element to specify **TableHeading** as a table heading
- Typing the **GeneralRule** for the **TableHeading** element's contents: one **TableRow** element

To define the **TableHeading** element:

1. Add an element definition to the EDD and tag it **TableHeading**.
   a. In the **Structure View**, click below the last **Element**.
   b. From the **Elements** panel, insert an **Element**.
      An **Element** and a **Tag** child element appear.
   c. In the **Tag** element, type: `TableHeading`

43

2. Define **TableHeading** as a **TableHeading** with a **GeneralRule** of **TableRow**.
   a. Click below the **Tag** element.
   b. From the **Elements** panel, insert **TableHeading**.
      **TableHeading** and a child **GeneralRule** element appear.
   c. In the **GeneralRule** element, type: `TableRow`
3. Save your changes.

You'll define the **TableRow** later, after defining a few other elements.

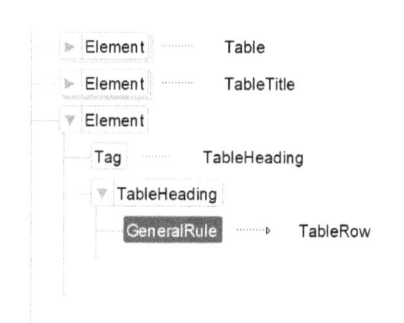

## Exercise 5: Defining a TableBody Element

In this exercise, you will define the **TableBody** element, by:
- Inserting an **Element** and typing the **Tag** as **TableBody**
- Inserting a **TableBody** element to specify **TableBody** as a table body
- Typing the **GeneralRule** for the **TableBody** element's contents: one or more **TableRow** elements

To define the **TableBody** element:
1. Add an element definition to the EDD and tag it **TableBody**.
   a. In the **Structure View**, click below the last **Element**.
   b. From the **Elements** panel, insert an **Element**.
      An **Element** and a **Tag** child element appear.
   c. In the **Tag** element, type: `TableBody`
2. Define **TableBody** as a **TableBody** with a **GeneralRule** of **TableRow+**.
   a. Click below the **Tag** element.
   b. From the **Elements** panel, insert **TableBody**.
      **TableBody** element and **GeneralRule** child element appear.
   c. In the **GeneralRule** element, type: `TableRow+`
3. Save your changes.

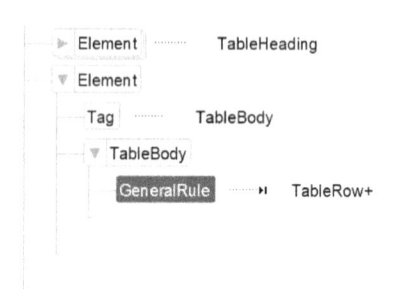

## Exercise 6: Defining a TableFooting Element

In this exercise, you will define the **TableFooting** element, by:

- Inserting an **Element** and typing the **Tag** as **TableFooting**
- Inserting a **TableFooting** element to specify **TableFooting** as a table footing
- Typing the **GeneralRule** for the **TableFooting** element's contents: one **TableRow** element

To define the **TableFooting** element:

1. Add an element definition to the EDD and tag it **TableFooting**.
   a. In the **Structure View**, click below the last **Element**.
   b. From the **Elements** panel, insert an **Element**.
      An **Element** and a **Tag** child element appear.
   c. In the **Tag** element, type: `TableFooting`
2. Define **TableFooting** as a **TableFooting** with a **GeneralRule** of **TableRow**.
   a. Click below the **Tag** element.
   b. From the **Elements** panel, insert **TableFooting**.
      **TableFooting** element and **GeneralRule** child element appear.
   c. In the **GeneralRule** element, type: `TableRow`
3. Save your changes.

## Exercise 7: Defining a TableRow Element

In this exercise, you will define the **TableRow** element, by:

- Inserting an **Element** and typing the **Tag** as **TableRow**
- Inserting a **TableRow** element to specify **TableRow** as a table row
- Typing the **GeneralRule** for the **TableRow** element's contents: one **Name**, one **Num**, one **Count**

To define the **TableRow** element:

1. Add an element definition to the EDD and tag it **TableRow**.
   a. In the **Structure View**, click below the last **Element**.
   b. From the **Elements** panel, insert an **Element**.
      An **Element** and a child **Tag** child element appear.
   c. In the **Tag** element, type: `TableRow`
2. Define **TableRow** as a **TableRow** with a **GeneralRule** of **Name, Num, Count**.
   a. Click below the **Tag** element.
   b. From the **Elements** panel, insert **TableRow**.
      A **TableRow** element and **GeneralRule** child element appear.
   c. In the **GeneralRule** element, type: `Name, Num, Count`

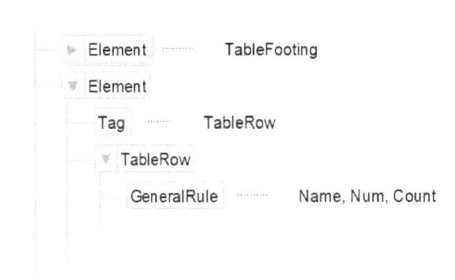

3. Save your changes.

**Exercise 8: Defining TableCell Elements**

In this exercise, you will define separate Name, Num, and Count table cell elements, with a general rule of <TEXT>

To define the **TableCell** elements:

1. Add an element definition to the EDD and tag it **Name**.
   a. In the **Structure View**, click below the last **Element**.
   b. From the **Elements** panel, insert an **Element**.
      An **Element** and a **Tag** child element appear.
   c. In the **Tag** element, type: `Name`
2. Define **Name** as a **TableCell** with a **GeneralRule** of <TEXT> 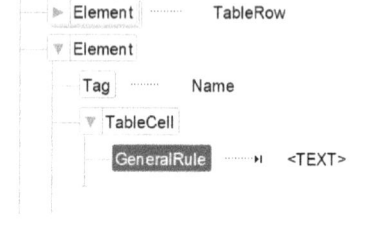
   a. Click below the **Tag** element.
   b. From the **Elements** panel, insert **TableCell**.
      A **TableCell** element and a **GeneralRule** child element appear.
   c. In the **GeneralRule** element, type: `<TEXT>`
3. Add an element definition to the EDD and tag it **Num**.
   a. In the **Structure View**, click below the last **Element**.
   b. From the **Elements** panel, insert an **Element**.
      An **Element** and a **Tag** child element appear.
   c. In the **Tag** element, type: `Num`

> Consider using **Copy/Paste** for duplicating similar structure

4. Define **Num** as a **TableCell** with a **GeneralRule** of <TEXT> 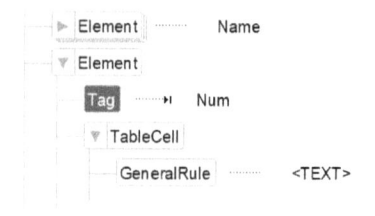
   a. Click below the **Tag** element.
   b. From the **Elements** panel, insert **TableCell**.
      A **TableCell** element and a **GeneralRule** child element appear.
   c. In the **GeneralRule** element, type: `<TEXT>`
5. Add an element definition to the EDD and tag it **Count**.
   a. In the **Structure View**, click below the last **Element**.
   b. From the **Elements** panel, insert an **Element**.
      An **Element** and a **Tag** child element appear.
   c. In the **Tag** element, type: `Count`

6. Define **Count** as a **TableCell** with a **GeneralRule** of <TEXT>
   a. Click below the **Tag** element.
   b. From the **Elements** panel, insert **TableCell**.
      A **TableCell** element and a **GeneralRule** child element appear.
   c. In the **GeneralRule** element, type: `<TEXT>`
7. Save your changes.

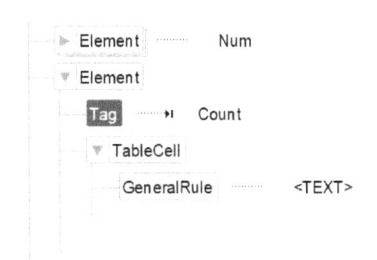

# Reimporting and Testing

### Exercise 9: Reimporting and Testing the Table

In this exercise, you will reimport the EDD into the structured template and test your element definitions for Section, Table, and child elements of Table.

1. Reimport your element definitions into your test document. If you had errors when importing the element definitions, correct your EDD and reimport.
2. Confirm that the changes you made to the EDD are working as expected.
3. In the **Structure View**, click on the line descending from any **Section** element but after a **Para** element.
4. From the **Elements** panel, insert a **Table** element.
   The **Insert Table** dialog appears.
5. In the **Insert Table** dialog, specify:
   - Columns: 3
   - Body Rows: 3
   - Heading Rows: 1
   - Footing Rows: 1
6. Click **Insert**.
   The **Document Window** shows the table.

The **Structure View** shows the table's overall structure, based on the number of rows and columns you specified.

Notice the invalid structure of each **TableRow** element.

Without a specific **InitialStructurePattern** rule to define initial table elements, by default, FrameMaker uses the first child element (**Name**) in the **GeneralRule** for **TableRow** and repeats that child element to create all the columns you specify in the **Insert Table** dialog.

Later, you will change this behavior by specifying an **InitialStructurePattern** for **TableRow**. In the meantime, you will change the **TableRow**'s child elements into the correct child elements.

7. Change the **Name** elements to **Num** elements where appropriate.
    a. In the **Structure View**, select the second **Name** element in the first **TableRow** in the **TableHeading**.
    b. From the **Elements** panel, select **Num** and click **Change**.
       **Name** changes to **Num**.
    c. Repeat for each additional **TableRow** in the **TableBody** and in the **TableFooting**.

8. Change the **Name** elements to **Count** elements where appropriate.
    a. In the **Structure View**, select the second **Name** element in the first **TableRow** in the **TableHeading**.
    b. From the **Elements** panel, select **Count** and click **Change**.
       **Name** changes to **Count**.
    c. Repeat for each additional **TableRow** in the **TableBody** and in the **TableFooting**.

9. Save your changes.

## Exercise 10: Testing the Parts of the Table

In this exercise, you will continue testing the parts of the Table—TableTitle, TableBody, TableHeading, TableFooting, TableRow, Name, Num, Count.

1. In the **Structure View**, click to the right of the **TableTitle** element and type:

   ```
   Items needing routine maintenance
   ```

2. Click in at least one of each—**Name**, **Num**, and **Count**— and enter text. (not shown)

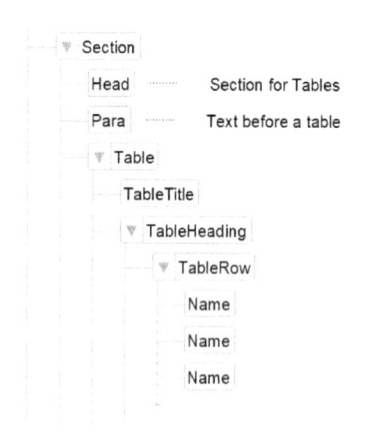

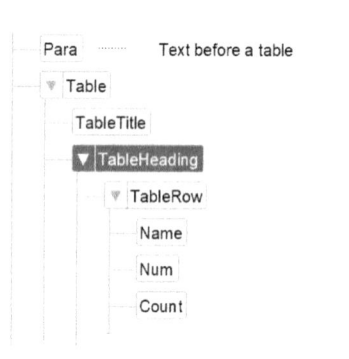

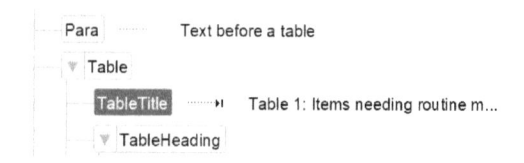

3. Add another row to the **TableHeading** in the **Document View**.

   a. Click in the heading row of the table.

   b. Press **Control-Return**.

   A second TableRow is added to TableHeading, but only one is allowed so the structure shows as invalid.

4. From the **Edit** menu, choose **Undo**.

   The invalid **TableRow** disappears.

5. Delete the **TableHeading**.

   a. In the **Structure View**, select the **TableHeading** element.

   b. Press **Delete**.

   The Clear Table Cells dialog appears.

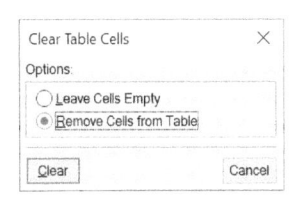

   c. Turn on **Remove Cells from Table**.

   d. Click **Clear**.

   The table heading is deleted.

   A TableHeading is required, so the structure is invalid.

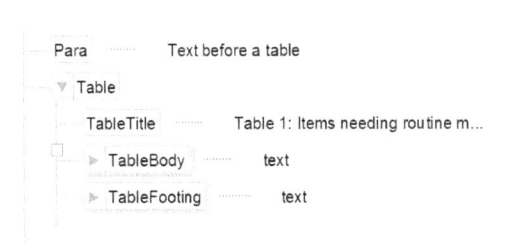

6. From the Edit menu, choose **Undo**.

7. Add another row to the TableFooting.

   a. Click in the footing row of the table.

   b. Press **Control-Return**.

   A second **TableRow** is added to **TableFooting**, but as with the TableHeading, only one is allowed so the structure is invalid.

8. From the **Edit** menu, choose **Undo**.

   The invalid **TableRow** disappears.

9. Delete the **TableFooting** element.

   a. In the **Structure View**, select the **TableFooting** element.

   b. Press **Delete**.

   The **Clear Table Cells** dialog appears.

   c. Turn on **Remove Cells from Table**.

   d. Click **Clear**.

The **TableFooting** disappears, and the structure is valid because the **TableFooting** is optional.

10. Save your changes.

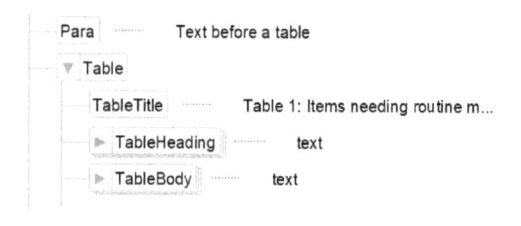

```
Para ········ Text before a table
▼ Table
    TableTitle ········ Table 1: Items needing routine m...
    ▶ TableHeading ········ text
    ▶ TableBody ········ text
```

# Chapter 5: Tables—InitialStructurePattern and InitialTableFormat

## Introduction

This chapter focuses on the **InitialStructurePattern** and **InitialTableFormat** for tables.

### Objectives

- Specify **InitialStructurePattern** for **Table** and table part elements
- Specify **InitialTableFormat** for **Table** element
- Reimport and test **InitialStructurePattern** and **InitialTableFormat**

### Overview of InitialStructurePattern

InitialStructurePattern is an optional part of element definitions for the following elements:

- Table
- TableHeading
- TableBody
- TableFooting
- TableRow

All tables have these common characteristics:

- Tables have at least a body
- Table heading, body, or footing elements have at least one row
- Table rows have same number of cells as columns in table

When you insert a Table element:

- You use **Insert Table** dialog to specify number of rows in heading, body, footing and number of columns
- FrameMaker automatically inserts necessary child elements to build a basic structure

If you do not specify initial structure, FrameMaker:

- Uses a default **GeneralRule** to give new table or table part its default initial structure
- Builds default initial structure by taking first of each type of table part in table's **GeneralRule**

You can use an InitialStructurePattern to specify:

- The **TableTitle, TableHeading, TableBody, TableFooting** elements that will initially appear in the table element
- The **TableRow** type elements that will appear in the **TableHeading, TableBody, TableFooting** type elements
- The **TableCell** type elements that will appear in the **TableRow** type elements

# Specifying an InitialStructurePattern

### Exercise 1: Specifying the InitialStructurePattern for a TableRow Element

In this exercise, you will define an **InitialStructurePattern** within the **TableRow** that will insert **Name, Num, Count** instead of inserting all **Name** elements.

1. If it is not already open, from your class files directory, open `EDD.fm`, the EDD you'll be modifying throughout the class.

   If you did not finish the previous chapter's modifications to the EDD, please open **Chapter 5-start Initial Table Format.fm** instead, and save it in your class files directory as `EDD.fm`.

   For instructions on downloading class files, see "Downloading class files" on page 1.

2. In the EDD, locate the **TableRow** element definition.
3. In the **Structure View**, click below **TableRow**'s **GeneralRule** element.
4. From the **Elements** panel, insert **InitialStructurePattern**.

   An **InitialStructurePattern** element appears.

5. In the **InitialStructurePattern** element, type: `Name, Num, Count`
6. Save your changes.

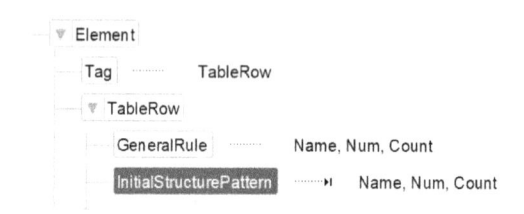

## InitialTableFormat—Overview

InitialTableFormat is an optional part of a Table element definition.

- It identifies which table format is preselected in the **Insert Table** dialog when user inserts **Table** element
- If no **InitialTableFormat** specified, **Table** element uses **Format A**
- Makes sure table format is consistent with **GeneralRule** for **Table** element

  If **Table** element's **GeneralRule** does not specify a **TableTitle** element, table format should not have one

**InitialTableFormat** is only a suggestion—user can change to another format without creating format override

You can specify a table format with a(n):

- **AllContextsRule**—wherever the element appears
- **ContextRule**—when element is in certain context
- **LevelRule**—when element is nested a specified number of levels in a specified ancestor

You'll learn more about context and level rules later in this course.

## Specifying the InitialTableFormat

### Exercise 2: Specifying the InitialTableFormat With an AllContextsRule

In this exercise, you will specify which table format will be preselected in the Insert Table dialog when the user inserts the Table elements.
The user can select a different table format without incurring a format rule override.

1. In the EDD, locate the Table element definition.
2. In the Structure View, click below Table's GeneralRule element.
3. From the Elements panel, insert InitialTableFormat.

   An InitialTableFormat element appears.

> At this point, you could specify a context-specific or level-specific rule. Since these rules are covered in the next chapter, you will insert the simpler AllContextsRule.

4. Insert AllContextsRule.

   An AllContextsRule element appears.

5. Insert TableFormat.

   A TableFormat element appears.

6. In the TableFormat element, type:
   ```
   Format B
   ```

7. Save your changes.

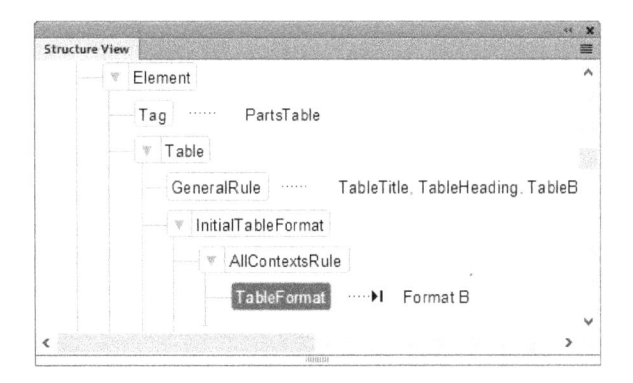

## Reimporting and Testing

### Exercise 3: Reimporting/Testing InitialStructurePattern and InitialTableFormat

In this exercise, you will reimport the EDD into the structured template and test your InitialStructurePattern on TableRow and InitialTableFormat on Table.

1. Reimport your element definitions into your test document. If you had errors when importing the element definitions, correct your EDD and reimport.
2. Confirm that the changes you made to the EDD are working as expected.
3. In the Structure View, click below a List element.

4. From the **Elements** panel, insert a **Para** element.
5. Click below the **Para** element.
6. Insert a **Table** element.

   The **Insert Table** dialog appears, with **Format B** preselected as you defined in the EDD.

7. In the **Insert Table** dialog, specify:
   - Columns: 3
   - Body Rows: 3
   - Heading Rows: 1
   - Footing Rows: 1

8. Click **Insert**.

   The **Document Window** displays the table.

   The **Structure View** displays the table's overall structure, based on the number of rows and columns you specified.

   Notice the valid structure of the **TableRow** elements which now contain **Name, Num, Count** as defined in the EDD, rather than three **Name** elements.

   By default, FrameMaker uses the first child element found in the **TableRow GeneralRule** (in this case, **Name**) and repeats that child element to create all the columns you specify in the **Insert Table** dialog. You changed this behavior by specifying an **InitialStructurePattern** for **TableRow**.

9. Save your changes.

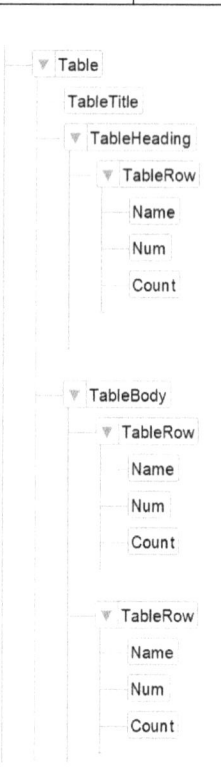

# Chapter 6: Inclusions and Exclusions

## Introduction

Inclusions allow elements to occur anywhere inside a defined element or its descendants. They are often used for infrequently used elements that might be necessary in multiple places within the hierarchy, such as **Footnote** or **Term**. Inclusions greatly simplify the general rules for elements. They also help your audience manage their **Elements** panel view by allowing you to list less critical elements at the bottom of the list of available elements via the **Elements** panel **Options** ( ). Set to display inclusions after other valid elements, the **Term** element in the screen capture to the right displays the inclusion icon ( ) and is listed after other valid elements.

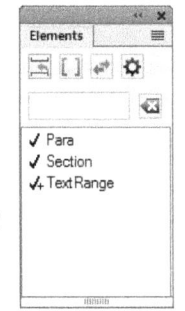

This chapter focuses on defining **Inclusions** and **Exclusions** for **Container**, **Footnote**, **Table** and table part elements.

## Objectives

- Specify use of an inclusion
- Define the included element
- Specify an exclusion of an element
- Reimport and test inclusions and exclusions

## Defining Inclusions

Inclusions are an optional part of element definitions for:

- Containers
- Table, TableTitle, TableHeading, TableBody, TableFooting, TableRow, TableCell
- Footnotes

### Exercise 1: Specifying Inclusions

In this exercise, you will define a new **Container** element tagged **Term** to contain the names of other documents mentioned throughout the chapters of the maintenance manuals. Rather than referencing **Term** in the **GeneralRule** for each element, you will define it as an inclusion for **Section**. **Term** can then be included anywhere within **Section** and its descendants.

1. If it is not already open, from your class files directory, open **EDD.fm**, the EDD you've been modifying throughout the class.

    If you did not finish the previous chapter's modifications to the EDD, please open **Chapter 6-start Inclusions Exclusions.fm** instead, and save it in your class files directory as `EDD.fm`.

For instructions on downloading class files, see "Downloading class files" on page 1.

2. In the EDD, create a new **Element** definition and tag it **Term**.
   a. In the **Structure View**, click below the last **Element** definition.
   b. From the **Elements** panel, insert a new **Element**.
      An **Element** and **Tag** child element appear.
   c. In the **Tag** element, type: **Term** 
3. Define **Term** as a **Container** with a **GeneralRule** of <TEXT>
   a. Click below the **Tag** element.
   b. From the **Elements** panel, insert **Container**.
      A **Container** element and **GeneralRule** child element appear.
   c. In the **GeneralRule** element, type: <TEXT>
4. In the **Structure View**, locate the **Section** element.
5. Click below the **GeneralRule** of the **Section** element.
6. From the **Elements** panel, insert **Inclusion**.
   An **Inclusion** element appears. 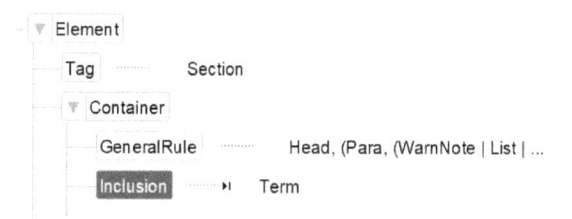
7. In the **Inclusion** element, type: Term
8. Save your changes.

You'll test this change after also defining an exclusion.

## Defining Exclusions

Exclusions are an optional part of element definitions for:
- **Container**
- **Table, TableTitle, TableHeading, TableBody, TableFooting, TableRow, TableCell**
- **Footnote**

Exclusions specify:
- Elements that cannot occur anywhere in a defined element or its descendants
- Exclusions are often used to negate inclusions

### Exercise 2: Specifying Exclusions

In this exercise, you will exclude **Term** from **Head** and **Table** so that it cannot appear within any **Head** element or any **Table** element or its descendant parts.

1. In the **Structure View**, locate the **Head** element definition.
2. Click below the **Head**'s **GeneralRule** element.
3. From the **Elements** panel, insert **Exclusion**.

   An **Exclusion** element appears.
4. In the Exclusion element, type: `Term`
5. In the **Structure View**, locate the **Table** element.
6. Click below the **Table**'s **GeneralRule** element.
7. From the **Elements** panel, insert **Exclusion**.

   An **Exclusion** element appears.
8. In the **Exclusion** element, type: `Term`
9. Save your changes.

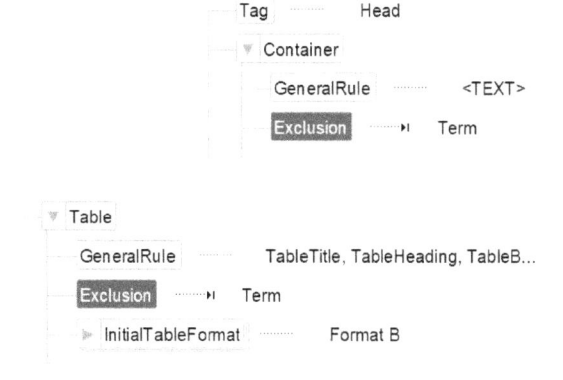

# Reimporting and Testing Inclusions and Exclusions

### Exercise 3: Reimporting and Testing Inclusions and Exclusions

In this exercise, you will reimport the EDD into the structured template and test your **Term** element and inclusions and exclusions.

1. Reimport your element definitions into your test document. If you had errors when importing the element definitions, correct your EDD and reimport.
2. Confirm that the changes you made to the EDD are working as expected.
3. In the **Structure View**, click anywhere on the line descending from the **Chapter** element.

   The **Elements** panel does not show **Term** as an inclusion, because you defined it as an inclusion on **Section**, not **Chapter**.
4. Click in the **Title** element.

   The **Elements** panel does not show **Term** as an inclusion, because you defined it as an inclusion on **Section**, and **Title** is a child of **Chapter**, not **Section**. 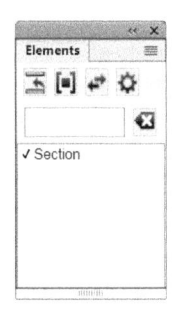
5. Click anywhere on the line descending from the **Section** element.

   The **Elements** panel shows **Term** as an inclusion. Your listed elements may differ depending on where you position your cursor in the structure view.
6. From the **Elements** panel, insert an **Term** element and insert some text.

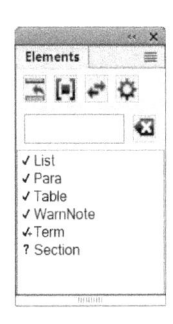

7. Insert an **Term** element in a Para element.
   a. Click in any **Para** element.
   b. Insert a **Term** element.
   c. Type some text.

   Note that the **Term** element forces a line break in the **Para** element. Later, you will define the **Term** element's formatting as a text range so that the break will disappear.

8. Click in any **Head** element.

   Although **Head** is a child of **Section**, the **Elements** panel does not show **Term** because you excluded **Term** from **Head**. (not shown)

9. Click in any **Num** element (in the table, not shown).

   Although **Num** is a descendant of **Section**, the **Elements** panel does not show **Term**, because you excluded **Term** from **Table** (and descendants of **Table**, like **Num**).

10. Save your changes.

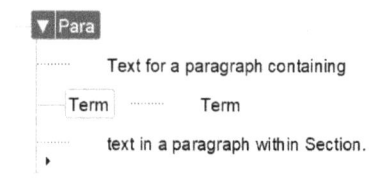

# Chapter 7: AutoInsertions

## Introduction

This chapter focuses on defining element **AutoInsertions** for **Container** elements.

### Objectives

- Specify autoinserted child elements
- Specify autoinserted nested child elements
- Reimport and test the AutoInsertions

### Overview of Autoinsertions

Autoinsertions are an optional part of element definitions for Container elements only

- They identify a child element to be inserted automatically with its parent
- Autoinsertions can also identify nested children ("grandchild" then "great-grandchild," etc.) to insert automatically
- Autoinsertions cannot automatically insert sibling elements

FrameMaker opens dialogs and windows as needed to specify:

- Attributes
- Table number of rows and columns
- Graphic positioning
- Cross-reference source
- Variable selection
- Marker text

## Specifying Autoinserted Child Elements

### Exercise 1:   Specifying Autoinserted Title Element

In this exercise, you will specify that the **Title** child element will appear automatically when you insert a **Chapter** element. When a first child element is required, specifying it as an **AutoInsertion** speeds up the authoring process.

1. If it is not already open, from your class files directory, open `EDD.fm`, the EDD you've been modifying throughout the class.

    If you did not finish the previous chapter's modifications to the EDD, please open **Chapter 7-start AutoInsertions.fm** instead, and save it in your class files directory as `EDD.fm`.

For instructions on downloading class files, see "Downloading class files" on page 1.

2. In the EDD, locate the **Chapter** element definition.
3. Click below the **Chapter**'s **GeneralRule** element (or click below the **ValidHighestLevel** element if you inserted it below, rather than above, the **Chapter**'s **GeneralRule**).
4. From the **Elements** panel, insert **AutoInsertions**.

    An **AutoInsertions** element with **InsertChild** element appear.
5. In the **InsertChild** element, type: `Title`
6. Save your changes.

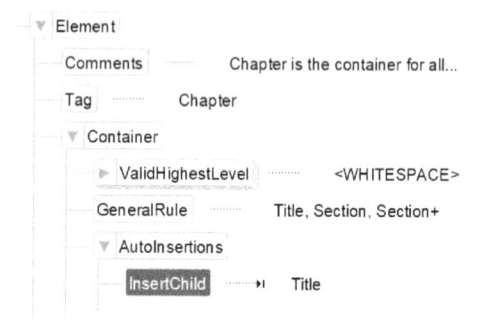

### Exercise 2:   Specifying Autoinserted Head Element

In this exercise, you will specify that the **Head** child element will appear automatically when you insert the **Section** element.

1. In the EDD, locate the **Section** element definition.
2. Click below the **Section**'s **Inclusion** element.
3. From the **Elements** panel, insert **AutoInsertions**.

    An **AutoInsertions** element with **InsertChild** element appear.
4. In the **InsertChild** element, type: `Head`
5. Save your changes.

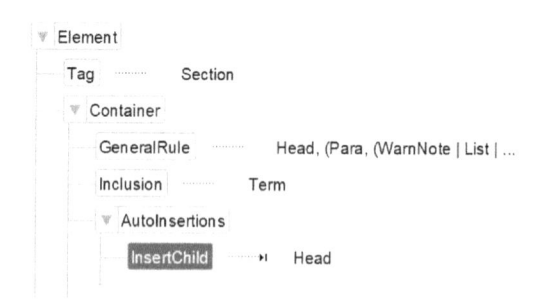

### Exercise 3: Reimporting and Testing Autoinserted Child Elements

In this exercise, you will reimport the EDD into the structured template, verify that **Allow Automatic Insertion of Children** is turned on, and test your **AutoInsertions** on **Chapter** and **Section**.

1. Reimport your element definitions into your test document. If you had errors when importing the element definitions, correct your EDD and reimport.
2. Confirm that the changes you made to the EDD are working as expected.
3. Verify that **Allow Automatic Insertion of Children** is turned on.

   Although **AutoInsertions** are defined in the EDD, the feature can be turned on and off in the document.

   a. Select **Element > New Element Options**.

   The **New Element Options** dialog appears.

   b. If not already on, turn on
   **Allow Automatic Insertion of Children**.

   c. Click **Set**.

4. In the **Structure View**, select and delete the **Chapter** element.

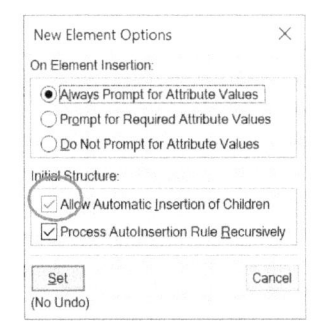

> Since **Chapter** is the highest-level element, all your test content disappears.
> (Yes, this is what you need to do!)

5. From the **Elements** panel, insert a **Chapter** element.

   The **Chapter** element appears, but this time is followed by a **Title** child element, courtesy of the **InsertChild** element in your EDD.

6. Type sample content into the **Title** element.
7. Click below the **Title** element.
8. Insert a **Section** element.

   A **Section** element appears, along with a child element of **Head**.

9. Type sample content into the **Head** element.
10. Save your changes.

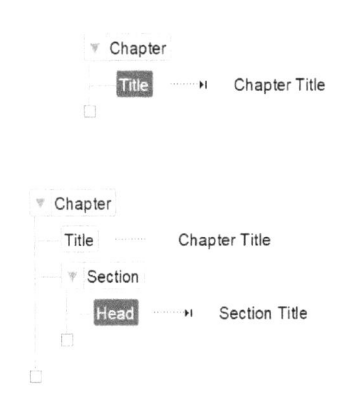

## Specifying Autoinserted Child and Nested Child Elements

### Exercise 4: Specifying Autoinserted Item and Nested Para Elements

In this exercise, you will redefine the **Item** element to contain one or more **Para** elements with optional **WarnNote** elements, rather than just <TEXT>. (In a later exercise, you will define formatting so that "first" and "not first" **Para** elements in Item elements have different formatting.)

After redefining **Item**, you will specify **AutoInsertions**:

- List will automatically insert **Item** child and **Para** nested child
- **Item** will automatically insert **Para** child

1. In the EDD, locate the **Item** element definition.
2. In the **Document Window**, replace the **GeneralRule** as follows:

   `(Para, WarnNote?)+`

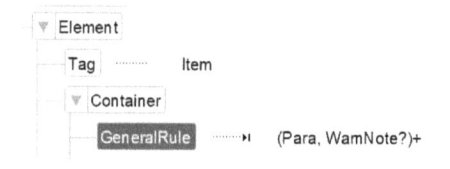

> Now, rather than allowing only a single paragraph of text (<TEXT>), an Item can now have multiple Para elements, along with optional WarnNote elements between paragraphs.

3. In the **Structure View**, locate the **List** element definition.
4. Click below the **List's GeneralRule** element.
5. From the **Elements** panel, insert **AutoInsertions**.

   **AutoInsertions** element with **InsertChild** element appear.
6. In the **InsertChild** element, type: `Item`
7. Click below the **InsertChild** element.
8. From the **Elements** panel, insert **InsertNestedChild**.

   An **InsertNestedChild** element appears.
9. In the **InsertNestedChild** element, type: `Para`

   Now, when you insert a **List** element, an **Item** child element and a nested **Para** child element will appear. However, this does not mean that when you insert an additional **Item** element, its **Para** child element will appear. To do this you will need to define an **Item** autoInsertion separately.

10. In the **Structure View**, locate the **Item** element definition.
11. Click below the **Item's GeneralRule** element.
12. From the **Elements** panel, insert **AutoInsertions**.

    An **AutoInsertions** element with **InsertChild** element appears.
13. In the **InsertChild** element, type: `Para`
14. Save your changes.

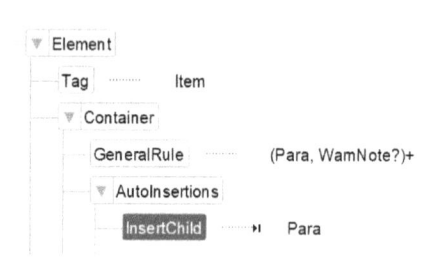

# Reimporting and Testing Item and Para Autoinsertions

**Exercise 5:   Reimporting and Testing Autoinserted Nested Child Elements**

In this exercise, you will reimport the EDD into the structured template and test your AutoInsertions on List and Item.

1. Reimport your element definitions into your test document. If you had errors when importing the element definitions, correct your EDD and reimport.
2. Confirm that the changes you made to the EDD are working as expected.

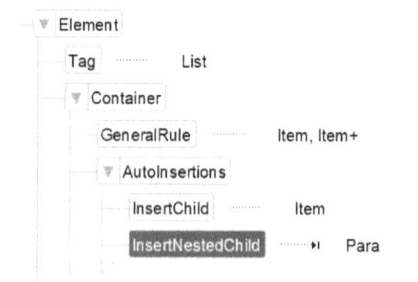

3. In the **Structure View**, click below the **Head** element.
4. From the **Elements** panel, insert a **Para** element.
5. Click below the **Para** element.
6. Insert a **List** element.

   **List** element and **Item** child element and **Para** nested child element appear.
7. Click below the **Item** element, on the line descending from the **List** element.
8. Insert an **Item** element.

   **Item** element and **Para** child element appear.
9. Save your changes.

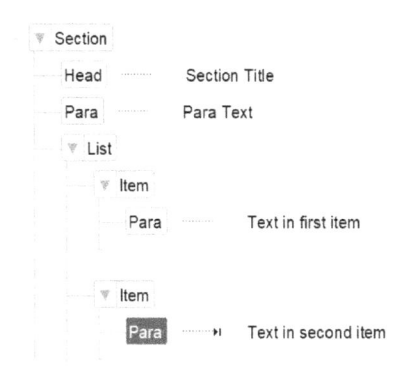

# Chapter 8: Defining and Formatting Objects

## Introduction

This chapter focuses on defining objects like cross-references, equations, graphics, and markers. These types of elements usually require formatting, using things like the **InitialObjectFormat** and the **SystemVariableFormatRule** for system variables.

## Objectives

- Define a **CrossReference** element (**XRef**) and specify its **InitialObjectFormat**, referring to a cross-reference format stored in a document
- Define an **Equation** element (**EQ**) and specify its **InitialObjectFormat**, referring to equation size
- Define a Figure element, which will contain both a **Caption** and **Graphic** element
- Define a **Graphic** element (**Graphic**) and specify its **InitialObjectFormat**, using the Import File or Anchored Frame dialog
- Define a **Marker** element (**IndexEntry**) and specify its **InitialObjectFormat**, referring to the marker type
- Define a **SystemVariable** element (**Date**) and specify its **SystemVariableFormatRule**, referring to variable name
- Reimport and test object elements and formats

## Overview of InitialObjectFormat

The **InitialObjectFormat** is an optional part of an object's element definition and specifies the default formatting applied when inserting an object.

The **InitialObjectFormat** is only a suggestion—an author can choose another format without creating format override.

| Object | InitialObjectFormat |
| --- | --- |
| **CrossReference** | Name of cross-reference format stored in the documents to be preselected in Cross-Reference dialog when user inserts element |
| **Equation** | Equation size of Small, Medium or Large |
| **Graphic** | ImportedGraphicFile or AnchoredFrame |
| **Marker** | Marker type to be preselected in Insert Marker dialog when user inserts element |

If **InitialObjectFormat** is not specified, FrameMaker applies defaults as follows:

| Object | InitialObjectFormat |
| --- | --- |
| **CrossReference** | Last Cross-Reference format chosen in dialog |
| **Equation** | Medium |
| **Graphic** | AnchoredFrame |
| **Marker** | Last marker type chosen in Insert Marker dialog or Marker window |

There are a number of ways to specify an **InitialObjectFormat**. You can specify a format with:

- **AllContextsRule**—wherever the element appears
- **ContextRule**—when element is in certain context
- **LevelRule**—when element is nested a specified number of levels in a specified ancestor

# CrossReference Elements

### Exercise 1:   Defining a CrossReference and InitialObjectFormat

In this exercise, you will:

- Redefine the **Para** element to contain optional **XRef** elements
- Define the **XRef** element as a **CrossReference**, using the **InitialObjectFormat** of **ElemNumTextPage**

The **InitialObjectFormat** for the **XRef** means that the **ElemNumTextPage** will be preselected in the **Cross-Reference** dialog when the user inserts the **XRef** elements. The user can select a different cross-reference format without incurring a format rule override.

1. If it is not already open, from your class files directory, open **EDD.fm**, the EDD you've been modifying throughout the class.

   If you did not finish the previous chapter's modifications to the EDD, please open **Chapter 8-start Define Format Objects.fm** instead, and save it in your class files directory as `EDD.fm`.

For instructions on downloading class files, see "Downloading class files" on page 1.

2. In the EDD, locate the **Para** element definition.
3. In the **Document Window**, change the **GeneralRule** as follows:

   (<TEXT> | Footnote | **XRef**)+

4. Create a new **Element** and tag it **XRef**.
   a. In the **Structure View**, click below the last **Element** definition.
   b. From the **Elements** panel, create a new **Element** definition.

      An **Element** and a **Tag** child element appear.
   c. In the **Tag** element, type: XRef
5. Define **XRef** as a **CrossReference**.
   a. Click below the **Tag** element.
   b. From the **Elements** panel, insert **CrossReference**.

      A **CrossReference** element appears.

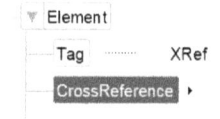

6. From the **Elements** panel, insert **InitialObjectFormat**.

   **InitialObjectFormat** element appears.

7. Insert **AllContextsRule**.

   **AllContextsRule** element appears.

8. Insert **CrossReferenceFormat**.

   **CrossReferenceFormat** element appears.

9. In the **CrossReferenceFormat** element, type: `ElemNumTextPage`

10. Save your changes.

## Exercise 2: Reimporting and Testing the Cross-Reference Element

In this exercise, you will reimport the EDD into the structured template and test your element definitions for **Para** and **XRef**.

1. Reimport your element definitions and fix any errors.

   a. In `testdoc.fm`, from the **File** menu, choose **Import > Element Definitions**.

      **Import Element Definitions** dialog appears.

   b. From the **Import from Document** popup menu, choose `EDD.fm`.

   c. Click **Import**.

      An alert box appears indicating "**Element definitions have been imported from the EDD**"

   d. Click **OK** to close the alert box.

      Because the format **ElemNumTextPage** does not exist, a FrameMaker log file appears, indicating that a format has been created for you. You will refine this format to meet your needs later in this exercise.

   e. Close the log file without saving it.

2. In the **Structure View**, click in any **Para** element.

3. From the **Elements** panel, insert an **XRef** element.

   If not already visible, the **Cross-Reference** panel appears with **ElemNumTextPage** preselected from the **Format** popup menu. The format was created for you on import, but the format's definition (displayed below the format name, circled in the screencapture) is empty.

   Next, you will edit the definition.

4. Click **Edit Format**.

   The **Edit Cross-Reference Format** dialog appears.

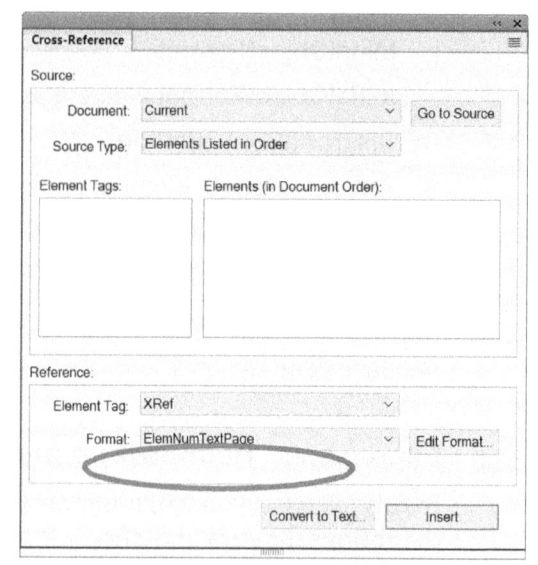

5. In the **Definition** text box, type:
   ```
   See <$elemparanum> <$elemtext>, on page <$elempagenum>.
   ```

6. Click **Change** to change the format.

   Note: Adding a leading space to a cross-reference format allows you to omit a leading space when inserting full-sentence cross-references.

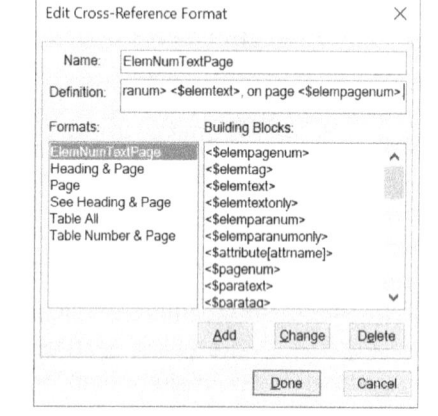

7. Click **Done** to dismiss the **Edit Cross-Reference Format** dialog.

   The **Update References** dialog appears.

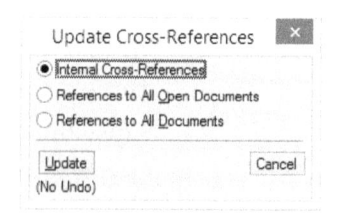

8. Click **Update** to update any references that have been inserted using the format.

   Note that the **Cross-Reference** panel is empty.

   Before you can successfully insert an element-based cross-reference, you need to define some attributes for the **XRef** element and the elements that will be referenced. You will do that in a later module. After adding attributes to your content model, you will be able to insert cross-references to **Title**, **Head**, **Figure**, and **Table** elements.

9. Save your changes.

> In your own work, consider storing the format of ElemNumTextPage in your EDD to make it easier to import the format (using File > Import > Formats) into your chapters.

# Equation Elements

### Exercise 3: Defining an Equation and Specifying Its InitialObjectFormat

In this exercise, you will:

- Redefine the **Section** element to contain optional **EQ** elements
- Define the **EQ** element as an **Equation**, using the **InitialObjectFormat** of **LargeEquation**

**LargeEquation** indicates the size of the characters in the equation, not the number of characters the equation can have. The user can specify a different equation size without incurring a format rule override.

1. In the EDD, locate the **Section** element definition.
2. In the **Document Window**, add **EQ** to the **GeneralRule** as follows:

   ```
   Head, (Para, (WarnNote | List | Table | EQ)?)+, (Section, Section+)?
   ```

3. Create a new **Element** and tag it **EQ**.

   a. In the **Structure View**, click below the last **Element** element.

   b. From the **Elements** panel, insert an **Element** element.

   An **Element** and a child **Tag** element appear.

   c. In the **Tag** element, type: EQ

4. Define **EQ** as an **Equation**.

   a. Click below the **Tag** element.

   b. From the **Elements** panel, insert **Equation**.

Equation element appears.

5. From the **Elements** panel, insert **InitialObjectFormat**.

    InitialObjectFormat element appears.

6. Insert **AllContextsRule**.

    AllContextsRule element appears.

7. Insert **LargeEquation**.

    LargeEquation element appears.

8. Save your changes.

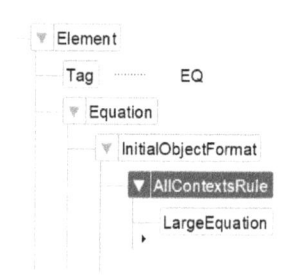

## Exercise 4: Reimporting and Testing the Equation Element

In this exercise, you will reimport the EDD into the structured template and test your element definitions for Section and EQ.

1. Reimport your element definitions into your test document. If you had errors when importing the element definitions, correct your EDD and reimport.
2. Confirm that the changes you made to the EDD are working as expected.
3. In the **Structure View**, click below a **Para** element in a **Section**.
4. From the **Elements** panel, insert an **EQ** element.

    An equation frame appears with the question mark (?) in the middle of the frame selected.

5. Click on the question mark to highlight it and type the following: x+x=2x

    [[Chapter Title]]
    [[Section Title]]
    [Para Text]

    $$x + x = 2x$$

    [[[Text in first item]]]

6. Save your changes.

# Graphic Elements

## Exercise 5: Defining a Graphic and Specifying Its InitialObjectFormat

In this exercise, you will:

- Redefine **Section** to contain optional **Figure** elements
- Redefine **Item** to contain optional **Figure** elements
- Define **Figure** as a container of **Caption** followed by **Graphic**, with an **AutoInsertion** of **Caption**
- Define **Caption** as a **Container** of <TEXT>
- Define **Graphic** as a **Graphic** with an **InitialObjectFormat** of ImportedGraphic

ImportedGraphic indicates that the **Import File** dialog, rather than the **Anchored Frame** dialog, will open when the **Graphic** element is inserted. The user can close the **Import File** dialog and use the **Anchored Frame** dialog without incurring a format rule override.

1. In the EDD, locate the **Section** element definition.
2. In the **Document Window**, add **Figure** to the **GeneralRule** as follows:

   `Head, (Para, (WarnNote | List | Table | EQ |` **`Figure`**`)?)+, (Section, Section+)?`

3. In the EDD, locate the **Item** element definition.
4. In the **Document Window**, rewrite and expand the **GeneralRule** for **Item** as follows:

   `(Para, (WarnNote |` **`Figure`**`)?)+`

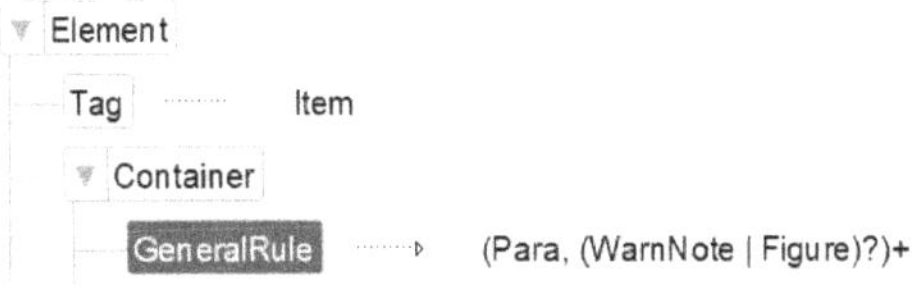

5. Create a new **Element** and tag it **Figure**.
   a. In the **Structure View**, click below the last **Element** element.
   b. From the **Elements** panel, insert an **Element** element.

      An **Element** and a child **Tag** element appear.
   c. In the **Tag** element, type: `Figure`
6. Define **Figure** as a **Container** of **Caption, Graphic**.
   a. Click below the **Tag** element.
   b. From the **Elements** panel, insert **Container**.

      **Container** element and **GeneralRule** child element appear.
   c. In the **GeneralRule** element, type: `Caption, Graphic`
7. Define **Figure** as having an **AutoInsertion** of **Caption**.
   a. Click below the **Figure**'s **GeneralRule** element.
   b. From the **Elements** panel, insert **AutoInsertions**.

      **AutoInsertions** element with **InsertChild** element appear.
   c. In the **InsertChild** element, type: `Caption`

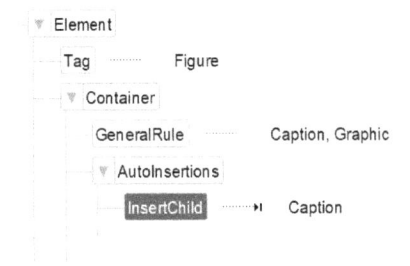

8. Create a new **Element** and tag it **Caption**.
   a. In the **Structure View**, click below the last **Element** element.
   b. From the **Elements** panel, insert an **Element** element.

      An **Element** and a child **Tag** element appear.
   c. In the **Tag** element, type: `Caption`
9. Define **Caption** as a **Container** of <TEXT>
   a. Click below the **Tag** element.
   b. From the **Elements** panel, insert **Container**.

      **Container** element and **GeneralRule** child element appear.
   c. In the **GeneralRule** element, type: `<TEXT>`

10. Create a new **Element** and tag it **Graphic**.
    a. In the **Structure View**, click below the last **Element** element.
    b. From the **Elements** panel, insert an **Element** element.
       An **Element** and a child **Tag** element appear.
    c. In the **Tag** element, type: `Graphic`
11. Define **Graphic** as a **Graphic**.
    a. Click below the **Tag** element.
    b. From the **Elements** panel, insert a **Graphic** element.
12. From the **Elements** panel, insert **InitialObjectFormat**.
    **InitialObjectFormat** element appears.
13. Insert an **AllContextsRule** element.
14. Insert an **ImportedGraphicFile** element.
15. Save your changes.

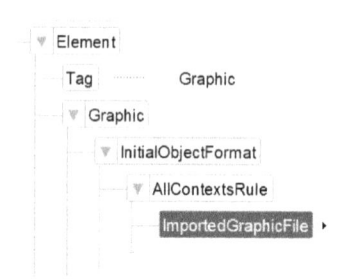

## Exercise 6: Reimporting and Testing the Graphic Element

In this exercise, you will reimport the EDD into the structured template and test your element definitions for **Section**, **Item**, **Figure**, **Caption**, and **Graphic**.

1. Reimport your element definitions into your test document. If you had errors when importing the element definitions, correct your EDD and reimport.
2. Confirm that the changes you made to the EDD are working as expected.
3. In the **Structure View**, create a new **Section** to test your **Figure** elements.
4. From the **Elements** panel, insert a **Figure** element.
   **Figure** element and **Caption** child element appear.
5. In the **Caption** element, type:
   `Caption for Figure`

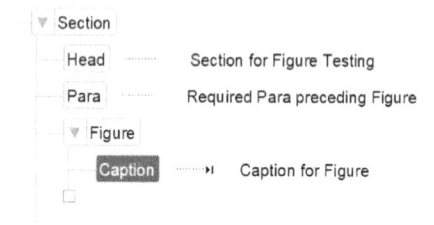

6. Click below the **Caption** element, on the line descending from the **Figure** element.
7. Insert a **Graphic** element.

   The **Import** dialog appears.
8. If necessary, change to your class files directory.
9. Select **sidedoor.tif**.
10. If necessary, select **Import by Reference**. 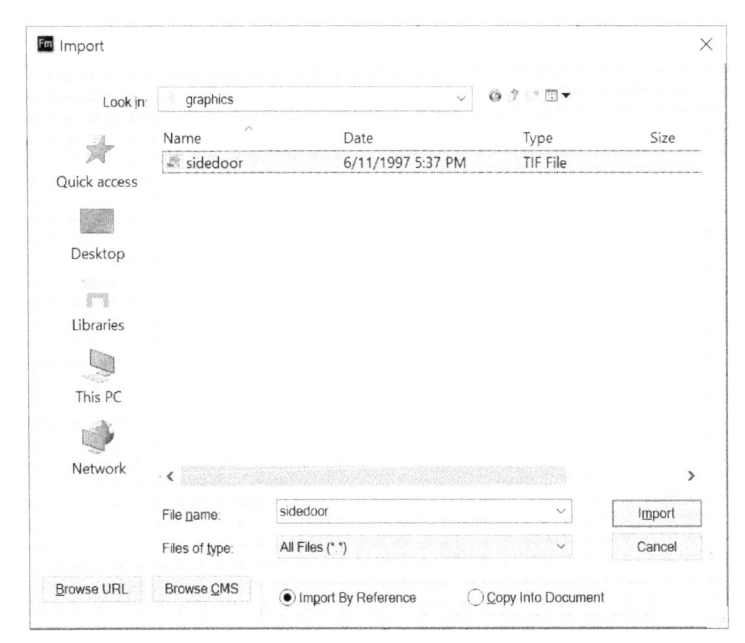
11. Click **Import**.

    The **Imported Graphic Scaling** dialog appears.
12. Select **150 dpi** and click **Set**.

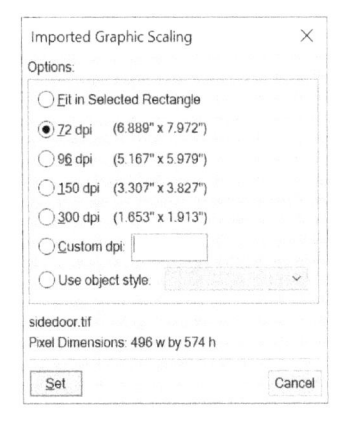

    The sample graphic appears below the caption, in an anchored frame sized to fit the graphic.
13. Click in any **Item** element but below a **Para** element.
14. Insert a **Figure** element and test by adding caption and **sidedoor.tif** as above.

    A **Figure** element with child elements appears.
15. Save your changes.

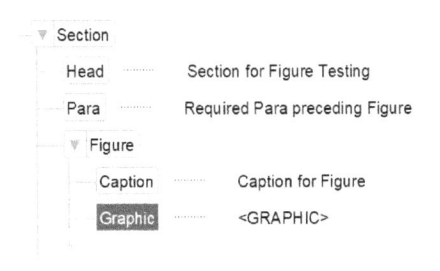

# Marker Elements

### Exercise 7: Defining a Marker and Specifying Its InitialObjectFormat

In this exercise, you will:
- Redefine the **Para** element to contain optional **IndexEntry** elements
- Define the **IndexEntry** element as a **Marker**, using the **InitialObjectFormat** of Index

**Index** will be the preselected marker type in the **Insert Marker** dialog when the user inserts the **IndexEntry** elements. The user can select a different marker type without incurring a format rule override.

1. In the EDD, locate the **Para** element definition.
2. In the **Document Window**, change the **GeneralRule** as follows:

   `(<TEXT> | Footnote | XRef | `**`IndexEntry`**`)+`

3. Create a new **Element** and tag it **IndexEntry**.
   a. In the **Structure View**, click below the last **Element** element.
   b. From the **Elements** panel, insert an **Element** element.

      An **Element** and a child **Tag** element appear.

   c. In the **Tag** element, type: `IndexEntry`
4. Define **IndexEntry** as a **Marker**.
   a. Click below the **Tag** element.
   b. From the **Elements** panel, insert **Marker**.
5. From the **Elements** panel, insert **InitialObjectFormat**.
6. Insert **AllContextsRule**.
7. Insert **MarkerType**.
8. Insert **Index**.
9. Save your changes.

## Exercise 8:  Reimporting and Testing the Marker Element

In this exercise, you will reimport the EDD into the structured template and test your element definitions for **Para** and **IndexEntry**.

1. Reimport your element definitions into your test document. If you had errors when importing the element definitions, correct your EDD and reimport.
2. Confirm that the changes you made to the EDD are working as expected.
3. In the **Structure View**, click in any **Para** element.
4. From the **Elements** panel, insert an **IndexEntry** element.

   The **Insert Marker** dialog appears with **Index** preselected from the **Marker Type** popup menu.

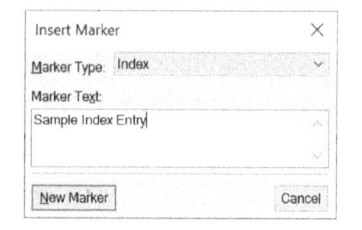

5. In the **Marker Text** dialog, type: `Sample index entry`
6. Click **New Marker**.

   In the **Structure View**, the **IndexEntry** element appears with "Sample index entry" to the right of the element bubble. Also, if you view your text symbols (**View>Text Symbols**) you will see a marker symbol ( **T** ) at the insertion point in the **Document Window**.

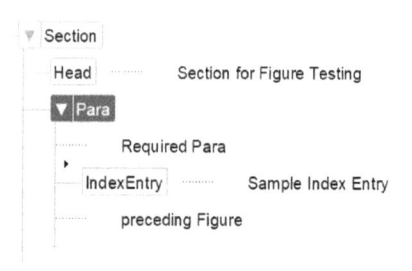

7. Save your changes.

# SystemVariableFormatRule

## A required part of definitions for SystemVariable elements

- Identifies which system variable to use
- A SystemVariableFormatRule is not a suggestion—users cannot change to another format without creating format override

## You can specify a SystemVariableFormatRule with:

- AllContextsRule—wherever the element appears
- ContextRule—when element is in certain context
- LevelRule—when element is nested a specified number of levels in a specified ancestor
- DefaultSystemVariable—uses FilenameLong system variable

### Exercise 9: Defining a System Variable and Specifying Its Format Rule

In this exercise, you will:

- Expand the **GeneralRule** for the **Para** element to contain a **Date** element
- Define the **Date** element as a **System Variable**, using the **SystemVariableFormatRule** of **CurrentDateLong**.

The **Current Date (Long)** system variable will be inserted when the user inserts the **Data** elements. The user *cannot* select a different system variable without incurring a format rule override.

1. In the EDD, locate the **Para** element definition.
2. In the **Document Window**, add **Date** to the **GeneralRule** as follows:

   `(<TEXT> | Footnote | XRef | IndexEntry | `**`Date`**`)+`

3. Create a new **Element** and tag it **Date**.
    a. In the **Structure View**, click below the last **Element** element.
    b. From the **Elements** panel, insert an **Element** element.
       An **Element** and a child **Tag** element appear.
    c. In the **Tag** element, type: `Date`
4. Define **Date** as a **SystemVariable**.
    a. Click below the **Tag** element.
    b. From the **Elements** panel, insert **SystemVariable**.
5. From the **Elements** panel, insert **SystemVariableFormatRule**.
6. Insert **AllContextsRule**.
7. Insert **UseSystemVariable**.
8. Insert **CurrentDateLong**.
9. Save your changes.

### Exercise 10: Reimporting and Testing the System Variable Element

In this exercise, you will reimport the EDD into the structured template and test your element definitions for **Para** and **Date**.

1. Reimport your element definitions into your test document. If you had errors when importing the element definitions, correct your EDD and reimport.
2. Confirm that the changes you made to the EDD are working as expected.
3. In the **Structure View**, click in any **Para** element.
4. From the **Elements** panel, insert a **Date** element.

   Today's date appears at the insertion point.
5. Save your changes.

# Chapter 9: Attribute List

## Introduction

This chapter focuses on defining attributes for elements in an **AttributeList**.

### Objectives

- Review uses of attributes
- Review basic types of attributes and their parts
- Specify the attribute **Name**
- Specify the attribute **Type**
- Indicate whether the attribute is **Optional** or **Required**
- Indicate whether the attribute is **ReadOnly**
- For attribute of numeric type (**Integer, Integers, Real, Reals**), define a **Range** of values
- For attributes of type **Choice**, define a list of **Choices**
- For attributes indicated as **Optional**, specify a **Default**

### Overview

#### Attributes are an optional part of all element definitions

- An **AttributeList** may contain one or more attributes
- Attributes can be used for general descriptions, cross-referencing, formatting, and prefixing

#### Potential attributes for metadata:

- A **Class** attribute of **Report** element could identify level of security
- A **Version** attribute of **Chapter** element might identify the current revision
- An **Author** attribute of **Section** element could identify the author of a portion of a document

#### Attributes for cross-referencing elements:

- Use a **UniqueID** type attribute for all elements to be cross-referenced, such as **Figure, Table, Title, Head**
- User can enter meaningful unique identification for element if not set to **ReadOnly**
- If **UniqueID** has a type attribute of **ReadOnly**, FrameMaker will autogenerate a value
- If **ReadOnly**, defining the **UniqueID** type attribute as **Optional** will prevent a "missing attribute value" validation error if element never referenced
- Use an **IDReference** type attribute for cross-reference elements (**XRef, TableXRef, FigXRef**) that refer to other elements
- Define **IDReference** type attribute as **Required** to force a link to a **UniqueID** attribute value for validity
- Define **IDReference** type attribute as **ReadOnly** if you don't want user to enter or edit the value

- If a referenced element has no **UniqueID** value, FrameMaker generates one and then copies generated **UniqueID** for **IDReference** attribute value

**Attributes used for formatting elements:**
Name/value attribute pairs in format rule can drive formatting of:
- Initial table format
- Initial object format
- System variable format
- Paragraph formatting
- Text-range formatting

**Attributes used for prefixing elements:**
Format rules can use attribute values to provide text for prefix or suffix:
- **Prefix** is text range that appears at beginning of element (before element's content)
- **Suffix** is text range that appears at end of element (after content)

# Basic Types of Attributes and Their Parts

Defaults can only be provided for attribute values defined as Optional (not Required). Plural attribute types (Strings, Integers, Reals) may have more than one default value

## Attribute Name

- Required part of all attribute definitions
- Type descriptive name of attribute
- Up to 255 characters, but better to keep concise
- Case-sensitive
- Cannot contain white space
- Cannot contain any of these special characters:
    ( ) & | , * + ? < > % [ ] = ! ; : { } "

## Attribute Type

- Required part of all attribute definitions
- Select one of predefined attribute types

## Optional or Required

- Required part of all attribute definitions
- Specify whether or not attribute requires value for each instance of element
- If attribute requires but does not have value, FrameMaker identifies attribute as invalid

## ReadOnly

- Optional part of all attribute definitions
- Specify whether to restrict users from entering and editing attribute value

## Range

- Optional part of attribute definitions for numeric types:
    Integer, Integers, Real, Reals
- Specify whether to restrict users to an inclusive range of values
    **Attributes** window displays range of values when this attribute is selected

## Choices

- **Choices** are a required part of attribute definitions for **Choice** attributes
- **Choices** are typed in manually in the **Choices** element
- The **Attributes** window displays choices in **Choices** popup menu when an attribute is selected
- **Choices**:
    - Can have labels up to 255 characters
    - Can have white-space characters
    - Cannot have any of these special characters:
        ( ) & | , * + ? < > % [ ] = ! ; : { } "

## Default

- Defaults are an optional part of attribute definitions for:
    **String** or **Strings**, **Integer** or **Integers**, **Real** or **Reals**, **Choice**
    But only if defined as **Optional** attribute value (not **Required**)
- Inserts a default value if user elects not to enter a value
- Can specify more than one default value for plural types (**Strings**, **Integers**, **Reals**)

# Defining attributes for metadata

### Exercise 1:  Defining a Required String Attribute

In this exercise, you will define a **Required String** attribute named **Author** for the **Chapter** element. To do this:

1. If it is not already open, from your class files directory, open `EDD.fm`, the EDD you've been modifying throughout the class.

    If you did not finish the previous chapter's modifications to the EDD, please open **Chapter 9-start Attributes.fm** instead, and save it in your class files directory as `EDD.fm`.

    For instructions on downloading class files, see "Downloading class files" on page 1.

2. In the EDD, locate the **Chapter** element definition.
3. Click below the **Chapter**'s **GeneralRule** element (or click below the **ValidHighestLevel** element if you inserted it below, rather than above, the **Chapter**'s **GeneralRule**).

4. From the **Elements** panel, insert **AttributeList**.

   An **Attribute** child element inserted automatically with a nested **Name** child element.

5. In the **Name** element, type: `Author`

6. Click below the **Name** element, on line descending from Attribute element.

7. From the **Elements** panel, insert **String**.

   A **String** element appears with insertion point below it.

8. From the **Elements** panel, insert **Required**.

9. Save your changes.

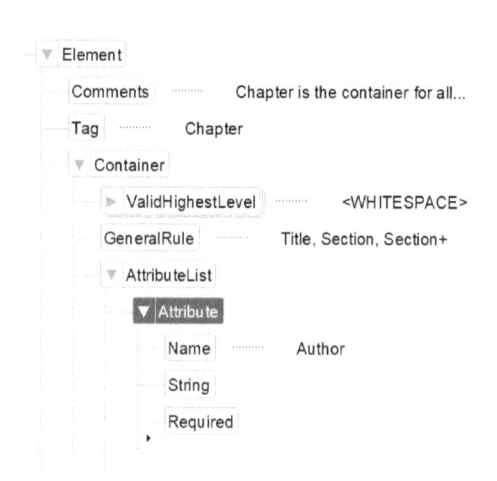

## Exercise 2:   Defining an Optional Real Attribute with a Range and Default

In this exercise, you will define an **Optional Real** attribute named **Version**, including a **Range** limitation and a **Default** value, for the **Chapter** element.

To do this:

1. In the EDD, locate the **Chapter** element definition.
2. In the **Structure View**, click below the **Author** attribute in the **AttributeList** element.
3. From the **Elements** panel, insert an **Attribute** element.

   A **Name** child element inserted automatically.

4. In the **Name** element, type: `Version`
5. Click below the **Name** element, on line descending from the **Attribute** element.
6. From the **Elements** panel, insert a **Real** element.
7. From the **Elements** panel, insert an **Optional** element.
8. From the **Elements** panel, insert **Range**.

   A **Range** element and **From** child element appear.

9. In **From** element, type: `1`
10. Click below the **From** element, on line descending from **Range** element.
11. From the **Elements** panel, insert a **To** element.
12. In the **To** element, type: `5`
13. Click below the **Range** element, on line descending from the **Attribute** element.
14. From the **Elements** panel, insert **Default**.
15. In the **Default** element, type: `1`
16. Save your changes.

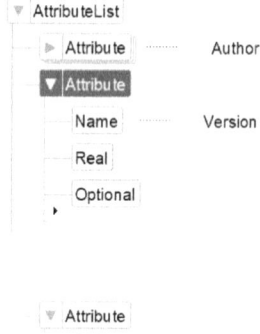

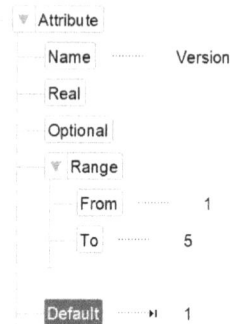

## Exercise 3: Reimporting and Testing Attributes

In this exercise, you will reimport the EDD into the structured template, verify that **Always Prompt for Attribute Values** is turned on, and test your attributes on **Chapter**.

1. Reimport your element definitions into your test document. If you had errors when importing the element definitions, correct your EDD and reimport.
2. Confirm that the changes you made to the EDD are working as expected.
3. Verify that **Always Prompt for Attribute Values** is turned on.

   The author can choose to be prompted for attribute values upon insertion of elements.

   a. From the **Element** menu, choose **New Element Options**.

   The **New Element Options** dialog appears.

   b. If not already on, turn on **Always Prompt for Attribute Values**.

   c. Click **Set**.

4. In the **Structure View**, select and delete the **Chapter** element.

   Since **Chapter** is the highest-level element, all the contents disappear.

5. From the **Elements** panel, insert a **Chapter** element.

   The **Attributes for New Element** dialog appears.

6. In the **Attribute Name** list, select **Author**.
7. Type a string value for the **Author** attribute and click **Set Value**.
8. In the **Attribute Name** scroll list, select **Version**.

   The dialog displays the properties of the **Version** attribute.

9. Type a number that is not between `1.0` and `5.0` and click **Set Value**.

   An alert appears, indicating your value is invalid.

10. Click **OK** to dismiss the alert.
11. Click **Insert Element**.

    The **Version** uses the default value of **1.0**.

12. Save your changes.

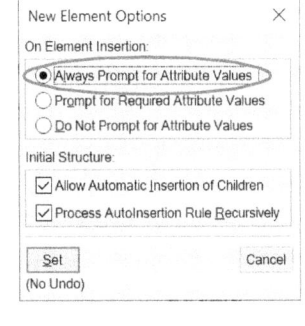

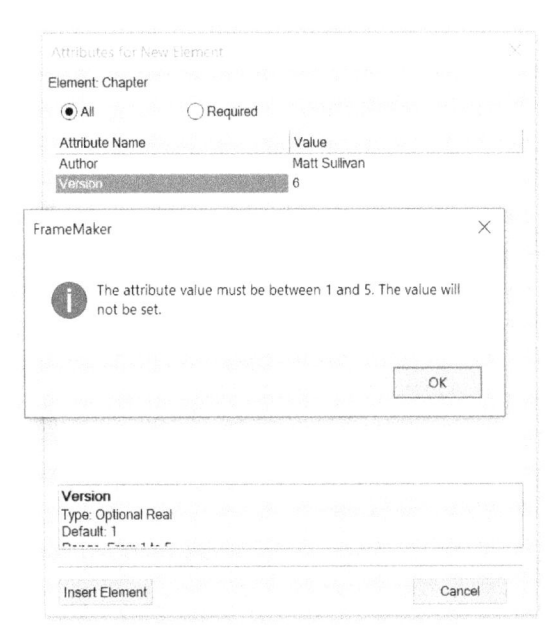

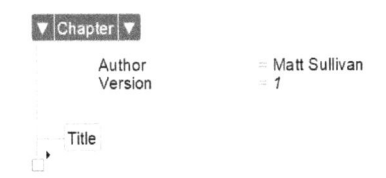

## Defining Attributes for Prefixes and Formatting

### Exercise 4: Defining an optional choice attribute to provide a prefix

In this exercise, you will define an optional choice attribute named **MessageType** with a **Default** value for the **WarnNote** element.

In a later exercise, you will use the value of the **MessageType** attribute to control the prefix of the **WarnNote** element.
To do this:

1. In the EDD, locate the **WarnNote** element definition.
2. In the **Structure View**, click below **WarnNote**'s **GeneralRule** element.
3. From the **Elements** panel, insert **AttributeList**.

   An **Attribute** child element inserted automatically with nested **Name** child element.

4. In the **Name** element, type: `MessageType`
5. Click below the **Name** element, on line descending from **Attribute** element.
6. From the **Elements** panel, insert **Choice**.

   A **Choice** element appears with insertion point below it.

7. From the **Elements** panel, insert **Optional**.

   An **Optional** element appears with insertion point below it.

8. From the **Elements** panel, insert **Choices**.

   A **Choices** element appears.

9. In the **Choices** element, type:
   `NOTE, WARNING`

10. Click below the **Choices** element, on the line descending from the **Attribute** element.

11. From the **Elements** panel, insert **Default**.

    A **Default** element appears.

12. In the **Default** element, type: `NOTE`
13. Save your changes.
14. Reimport your element definitions into your test document. If you had errors when importing the element definitions, correct your EDD and reimport.
15. Confirm that the changes you made to the EDD are working as expected.

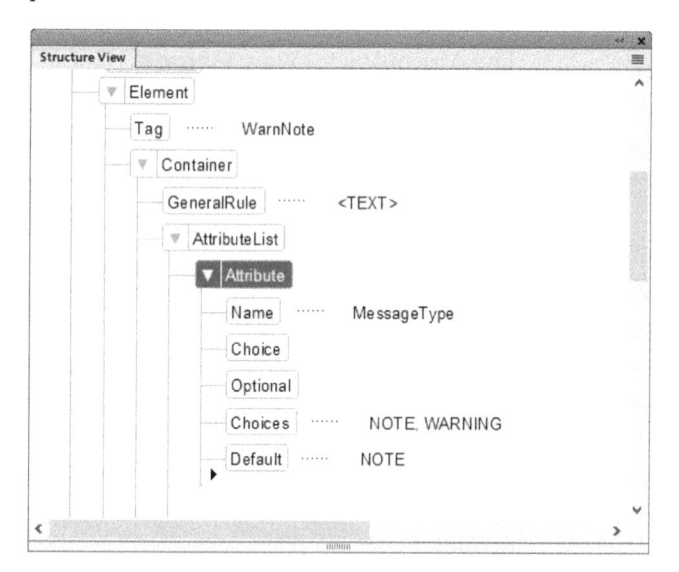

16. From the **Elements** panel, insert **Section**, **Head**, and **Para** elements to fill out structure requirements.

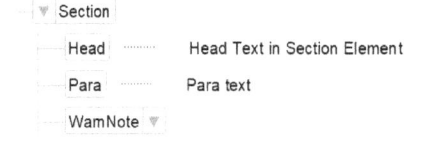

17. From the **Elements** panel, insert a **WarnNote**.

    The **Attributes for New Element** dialog appears.

18. In the **Attribute Name** scroll list, select **MessageType**.

    The dialog displays the properties of the **MessageType** attribute.

19. From the attribute value **Choices** popup menu, select WARNING and click **Insert Element**.

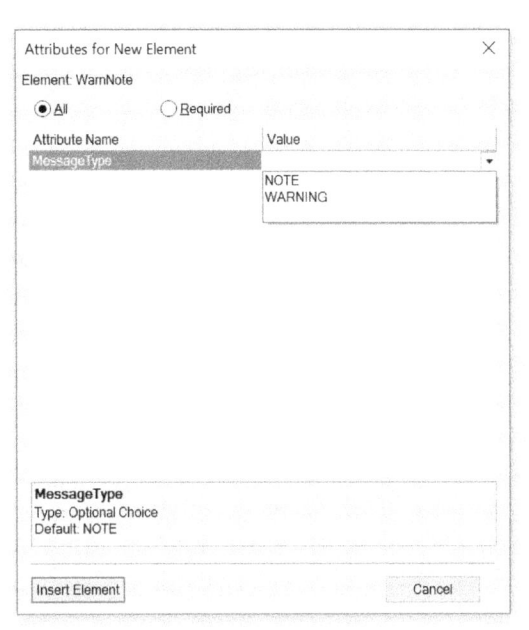

20. Click **Insert Element**.

    The **Structure View** displays the **MessageType** value. You will use this attribute value later as a prefix for your content.

21. Insert text into the **WarnNote** element.

22. Save your changes.

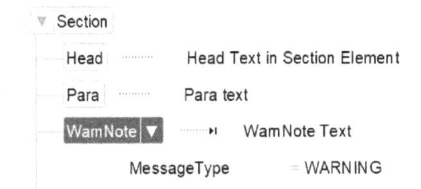

## Exercise 5: Defining an Optional Choice Attribute to Provide Formatting

In this exercise, you will define an optional choice attribute named **ListType** for the **List** element and include **Choices** and a **Default** value.

In a later exercise, you will use the value of the **ListType** attribute to control the formatting of the children of the **List** element.

To do this:

1. In the EDD, locate the **List** element definition.
2. In the **Structure View**, click below the **GeneralRule** for the **List** element.
3. From the **Elements** panel, insert an **AttributeList**.

    An **Attribute** child element is inserted, along with an automatically nested **Name** child element.

4. In the **Name** element, type: `ListType`
5. Click below the **Name** element, on line descending from **Attribute** element.

6. Insert a **Choice** element.
7. Insert an **Optional** element.
8. Insert **Choices**.
9. In the **Choices** element, type: `Bulleted, Numbered`
10. Click below **Choices** element, on line descending from **Attribute** element.
11. Insert **Default**.

    A **Default** element appears.
12. In the Default element, type: `Bulleted`
13. Save your changes.
14. Reimport your element definitions into your test document. If you had errors when importing the element definitions, correct your EDD and reimport.
15. Confirm that the changes you made to the EDD are working as expected.
16. From the **Elements** panel, insert a **Para** with text at the end of your section.
17. Place your cursor below the **Para** element and insert a **List** element.

    The **Attributes for New Element** dialog appears.
18. In the **Attribute Name** scroll list, select **ListType**.
19. From the attribute value **Choices** popup menu, select **Numbered** and click **Insert Element**.

    You will set numbering for this list in another lesson.
20. Click **Insert Element**.

    The **Structure View** displays the attribute value.
21. Save your changes.

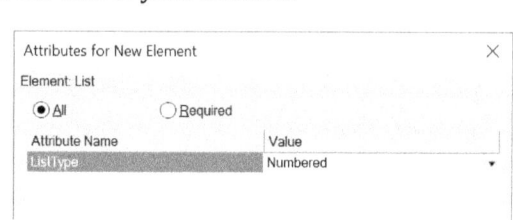

## Exercise 6: Defining an optional choice attribute to provide InitialObjectFormat

In this exercise, you will define an optional choice attribute named **ReadyToImport** for the **Figure** element and include choices and a default value.

In a later exercise, you will use the value of the **ReadyToImport** attribute to control the appearance of the **Import File** dialog or **Anchored Frame** dialog when inserting the **Figure** element's child **Graphic** element.

To do this:

1. In the EDD, locate the **Figure** element definition.
2. In the **Structure View**, click below **Figure**'s **GeneralRule** element.
3. From the **Elements** panel, insert **AttributeList**.

    An **Attribute** child element inserted automatically with nested **Name** child element.

4. In the Name element, type: **ReadyToImport**
5. Click below the **Name** element, on line descending from **Attribute** element.
6. Insert **Choice**.
7. Insert **Optional**.
8. Insert **Choices**.
9. In the **Choices** element, type: `Yes, No`
10. Click below **Choices** element, on line descending from **Attribute** element.
11. Insert **Default**.
12. In the **Default** element, type: `No`
13. Save your changes.
14. Reimport your element definitions into your test document. If you had errors when importing the element definitions, correct your EDD and reimport.
15. Confirm that the changes you made to the EDD are working as expected.
16. Add a **Para** element to the end of your **Section**.
17. From the **Elements** panel, insert a **Figure** element.

    The **Attributes for New Element** dialog appears.

18. In the **Attribute Name** scroll list, select **ReadyToImport**.
19. From the attribute value **Choices** popup menu, select **Yes**.
20. Click **Insert Element**.

    The **Structure View** displays the **ReadyToImport** attribute value.

21. Save your changes.

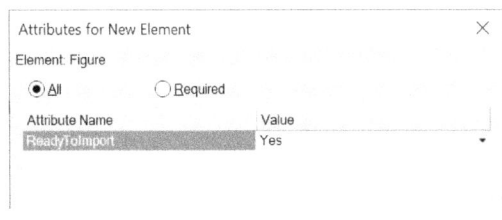

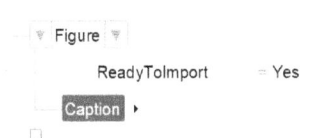

## Defining Attributes for Cross-Referencing

### Exercise 7: Defining an Optional, ReadOnly UniqueID Attribute for a Source

In this exercise, you will set up attributes for cross-referencing by creating an attribute with a **ReadOnly** specification named **ID** for the **Title**, **Head**, **Table**, and **Figure** elements.

In a later exercise, you will use the value of the **ID** for cross-referencing.

To do this:

1. In the EDD, locate the **Title** element definition.
2. In the **Structure View**, click below **GeneralRule** for **Title**.
3. From the **Elements** panel, insert **AttributeList**.

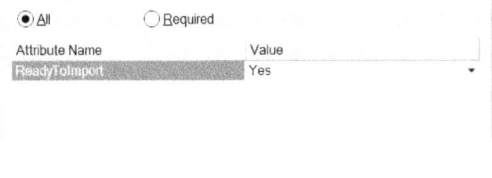

Nested **AttributeList**, **Attribute**, and **Name** elements are inserted automatically.

4. In the **Name** element, type: `ID`
5. Click below the **Name** element, on line descending from **Attribute** element.
6. Insert **UniqueID**.
7. Insert **Optional**.
8. Insert a **Special Attribute Controls** element below **Optional**.
9. Insert a **ReadOnly** element as a child of **SpecialAttributeControls**
10. Save your changes.
11. Repeat for the **Head** element.
    a. In the EDD, locate the **Head** element definition.
    b. In the **Structure View**, click below the **Exclusion** element in the **Head** element definition.
    c. From the **Elements** panel, insert **AttributeList**.
    
    Nested **AttributeList**, **Attribute**, and **Name** elements are inserted automatically.
    
    d. In the **Name** element, type: `ID`
    e. Click below the **Name** element, on line descending from **Attribute** element.
    f. Insert **UniqueID**.
    g. Insert **Optional**.
    h. Insert **ReadOnly**.
    i. Save your changes.

You can use Copy/Paste to speed definition of common attribute lists and individual attributes.

12. Repeat for the **Table** element.

13. Repeat for the **Figure** element.

    Since already has an **AttributeList** element, you will add the **ID** attribute as a child to the existing **AttributeList** element.

14. Save your changes.

15. Reimport your element definitions into your test document. If you had errors when importing the element definitions, correct your EDD and reimport.

16. Confirm that the changes you made to the EDD are working as expected.

17. From the **Elements** panel, inspect one each of **Title**, **Head**, **Table** and **Figure** elements. Insert elements as needed if they don't yet exist.

    Each element now has the **ID** attribute, which will populate when cross-referenced.

18. Save your changes.

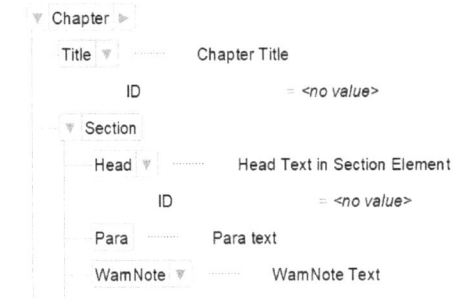

## Exercise 8: Defining a Required, ReadOnly IDReference attribute for XRef

In this exercise, you will define a required attribute named **IDRef**, including a **ReadOnly** specification, for the **XRef** element.

To do this:

1. In the EDD, locate the **XRef** element definition.

2. In the **Structure View**, click above **XRef**'s **InitialObjectFormat** element.

3. From the **Elements** panel, insert **AttributeList**.

   The **Attribute** child element inserted automatically with a nested **Name** child element.

4. In the **Name** element, type: `IDRef`

5. Click below the **Name** element, on line descending from **Attribute** element.

6. Insert **IDReference**.

   **IDReference** element appears with insertion point below it.

7. Insert **Required**.

   A **Required** element appears with insertion point below it.

8. Insert **ReadOnly**.

   **ReadOnly** element appears.

9. Save your changes.

10. Reimport your element definitions into your test document. If you had errors when importing the element definitions, correct your EDD and reimport.

11. Confirm that the changes you made to the EDD are working as expected.

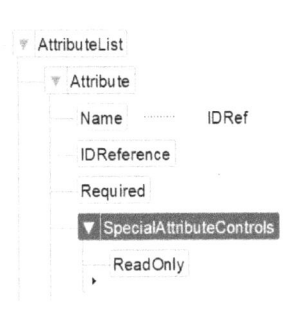

12. Position your cursor in a **Para** element.
13. From the **Elements** panel, insert an **XRef** element.

    The **Cross-Reference** dialog appears.

14. From the **Source Type** popup menu, choose **Elements Listed in Order**.

    The **Source Type** scroll list displays all element tags with an attribute of type UniqueID:
    - Figure
    - Head
    - Table
    - Title

15. From the **Source Type** scroll list, select **Head**.

    The **Source Text** scroll list displays all occurrences of the **Head** element in the document.

16. In the **Source Text** scroll list, select any one of your **Head** elements.

    **ElemNumTextPage** is already chosen from the **Format** popup menu, because you defined it as the **InitialObjectFormat** for **XRef**.

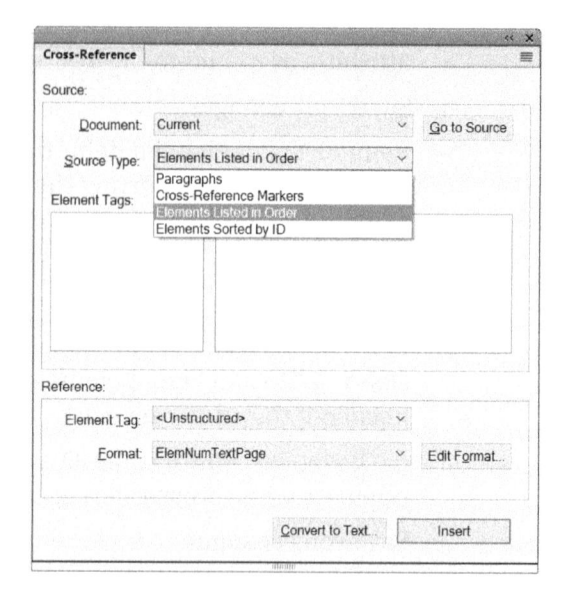

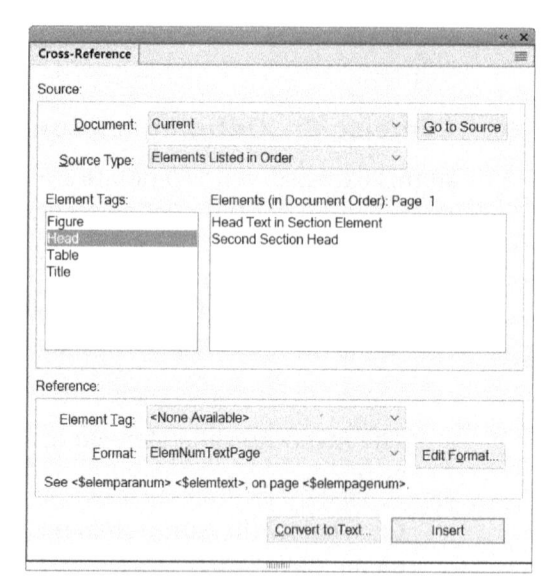

17. Click **Insert**.

    The cross-reference appears.

    Before inserting the **XRef** element, the **Section Head** had no **IDRef**.

    After insertion, the **Head ID** and corresponding **XRef IDRef** attributes have matching values.

    FrameMaker supplied the value for the **UniqueID** attribute because it was set to **ReadOnly** in the EDD.

18. Using the previous steps, insert **XRef** elements to **Title**, **Table** and **Figure** elements.

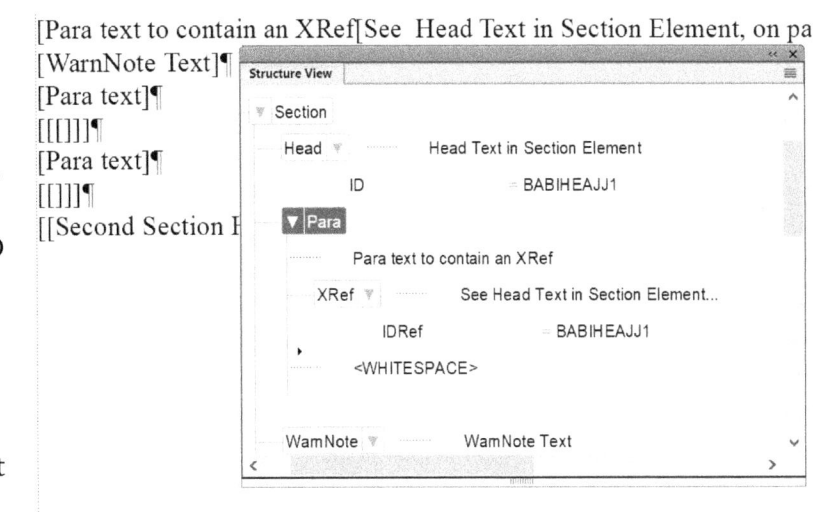

> You need to have at least one element of a given type in your document before you can insert a cross-reference to that type of element.

19. Save your changes.

# Chapter 10: AllContext formatting rules

## Introduction

This chapter focuses on writing the **TextFormatRules** for **Container**, **Footnote**, **Table** and table part elements.

## Objectives

- Define parts of text format rules
- Specify an **ElementPgfFormatTag**
- Write an:
    - AllContextsRule
    - **ContextRule** with If, ElseIf, Else clauses
    - **LevelRule** with If, ElseIf, Else clauses
- Refer to:
    - **ParagraphFormatTag** and **CharacterFormatTag**
    - Individual paragraph/text-range properties
    - **FormatChangeListTag**
- Analyze syntax for naming ancestors, siblings and attribute values
- Define subRules and multiple rules
- Write a **ContextLabel**
- Define a **FormatChangeList/FormatChangeListLimits**

## Overview

### AllContext rules are an optional part of element definitions for:

- Container
- Table, TableTitle, TableHeading, TableBody, TableFooting, TableRow, TableCell
- Footnote

### AllContext rules provide formatting for text in elements:

- Rules for **Table, TableHeading, TableBody, TableFooting, TableRow** specify formatting only for text in descendant **TableTitle** and **TableCell** elements
- Changes are considered overrides
- When a user imports element definitions into a document, they can keep or remove overrides

91

# The parts that make up TextFormatRules

| Part | Description |
|---|---|
| **ElementPgfFormatTag** | • Optional, zero or one, before other parts<br>• "Named" base paragraph format stored in document<br>• Defines all aspects of text and paragraph formatting—basic, default font, pagination, numbering, advanced, table cell |
| **AllContextsRule** | • Optional, zero or more, in any order<br>• Formatting change wherever the element appears |
| **ContextRule** | • Optional, zero or more, in any order<br>• With separate clauses:<br>  If—one<br>  ElseIf—zero or more<br>  Else—zero or one<br>• Formatting change when element is in certain context |
| **LevelRule** | • Optional, zero or more, in any order<br>• With separate clauses:<br>  If—one<br>  ElseIf—zero or more<br>  Else—zero or one<br>• Formatting change when element is nested a specified number of levels in an ancestor |

## Each AllContextsRule, and If/ElseIf/Else clause in ContextRule and LevelRule can refer to:

- A named **ParagraphFormatTag** or **CharacterFormatTag**
- Individual formatting properties
- A **FormatChangeList**

## Text formatting is hierarchical:

- An element can inherit properties from ancestors
- An element can pass on properties to descendants

## First, FrameMaker determines which base paragraph format to apply:

- If element's definition specifies base paragraph format, that format is used
- If not, FrameMaker searches up through ancestors until it finds element with format and uses that format
- If reaches top of element's hierarchy without finding a format, uses default Body paragraph format

## Second, determines formatting changes to apply:
- Goes back down through hierarchy to current element, cumulatively picking up formatting changes
- Changes can specify either:
    - Absolute values (fixed value, such as indent expressed as distance from left margin)
    - Relative values (change to current setting, such as amount to move indent)

## If the current element is in a table:
- Formatting will not search beyond an ancestor **Table** element
- If no ancestors prior to **Table** element specify paragraph format, the paragraph format stored in the table format will be used

## For text in a footnote element:
- No cascade beyond ancestor **Footnote** element
- If no paragraph formatting is specified within **Footnote** element, main flow footnotes will use the document's current footnote paragraph format and table footnotes will use the current table footnote paragraph format

## If document is part of book:
- If FrameMaker does not find paragraph format in document (when searching outside **Table** or **Footnote**) FrameMaker will continue looking for a paragraph format in ancestor elements of book files
- If found in book hierarchy, FrameMaker uses that paragraph format
- If FrameMaker reaches top of book without finding paragraph format FrameMaker uses the default **Body** paragraph format stored in document
- When using paragraph format from hierarchy in book, FrameMaker goes back down through hierarchy to current element, cumulatively picking up formatting changes

# Specifying the ElementPgfFormatTag

## Reference to "named" base paragraph format stored in document
- Defines all properties of text and paragraph formatting—basic, default font, pagination, numbering, advanced, table cell
- If instance of element contains text, text's format is paragraph format plus any changes specified for current context in element's format rules
- Paragraph format is also passed on to element's descendants—until descendant provides different format
- Rules for **Table**, **TableHeading**, **TableBody**, **TableFooting**, **TableRow** specify formatting only for text in descendant **TableTitle** and **TableCell** elements

### Exercise 1: Specifying a Base Tag for the Entire Flow

In this exercise, you will specify an **ElementPgfFormatTag** of **Body** for the **Chapter** element.

The paragraph tag **Body** will be inherited by all elements in the entire structure, unless another element specifies its own paragraph tag. Any individual format changes (such as a weight of bold or size of 14 points) defined in **Chapter** or its descendants will make changes to the properties defined in and inherited from the **Body** paragraph tag.

To do this:

1. If it is not already open, from your class files directory, open `EDD.fm`, the EDD you'll be modifying throughout the class.

   If you did not finish the previous chapter's modifications to the EDD, please open **Chapter 10-start Formatting.fm** instead, and save it in your class files directory as `EDD.fm`.

   For instructions on downloading class files, see "Downloading class files" on page 1.

2. In the EDD, locate the **Chapter** element definition.
3. In the **Structure View**, click below **AutoInsertions** for the **Chapter** element.
4. From the **Elements** panel, insert **TextFormatRules**.

   A **TextFormatRules** element appears.
5. Insert an **ElementPgfFormatTag**.

   An **ElementPgfFormatTag** element appears.
6. In **ElementPgfFormatTag** element, type: `Body`
7. Save your changes.
8. Reimport your element definitions into your test document. If you had errors when importing the element definitions, correct your EDD and reimport.
9. Confirm that the changes you made to the EDD are working as expected.

All elements now explicitly use the **Body** paragraph format.

## Understanding an AllContextsRule

An AllContextsRule specifies format that will apply to an element in all the contexts in which that element can occur. It can refer to:

- A **ParagraphFormatTag** (or **CharacterFormatTag** if a text range) stored in the document
- Individual paragraph or text-range formatting properties
- A **FormatChangeList**

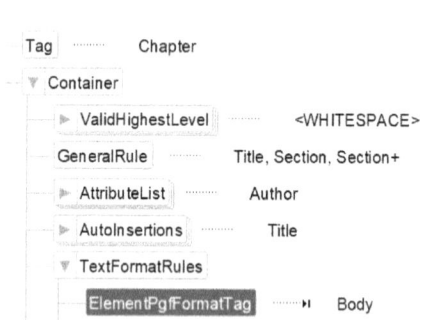

When an **AllContextsRule** refers to individual formatting properties, clauses can describe changes to any property in either the **Paragraph Designer** (except **Next Paragraph Tag**, which is not used in structured documents) or the **Character Designer** (which is basically the same as **PropertiesFont** properties of the Paragraph Designer. Here is an overview of property organization:

| | |
|---|---|
| **PropertiesBasic** | Set indentation, line spacing, paragraph alignment, paragraph spacing, and tab stops |
| **PropertiesFont** | Set font, size, and style of text in element |
| **PropertiesPagination** | Define placement of paragraph on page and determine how to break paragraph across columns and pages |
| **PropertiesNumbering** | Specify syntax and format for automatically generated string, such as number that appears at beginning of procedure step |
| **PropertiesAdvanced** | Set hyphenation and word spacing options and determine whether to display graphic with paragraph |
| **PropertiesTableCell** | Customize margins of cells and vertical alignment of text in them |

Some properties accept directly typed values, while other also allow insertion of keyword child element (such as **Bold** or **Yes**)

With some numeric values, you can type either:

- Relative values (positive or negative)—added to current value to set new value
- Absolute values—overrides current value for property

# FormatChangeList

You can use a **FormatChangeList** to:

- Describe set of changes to format properties
- Prevent repeat typing of same changes used throughout EDD

You can refer to a **FormatChangeList** by name in:

- Text format rules—**AllContextsRule**, **ContextRule**, **LevelRule**
- **PrefixRules** or **SuffixRules**
- **FirstParagraphRules** or **LastParagraphRules**

### Exercise 2:  Specifying an AllContextsRule Referring to "Basic" Properties

In this exercise, you will specify an **AllContextsRule** for the **Chapter** element, that specifies the space above and below the element. These changes to **Chapter** will be inherited by all elements in the entire structure, unless changed by another element's formatting.

To do this:

1. In the EDD, locate the **Chapter** element definition.
2. In the **Structure View**, click below the **ElementPgfFormatTag** of the **Chapter** element, on the line descending from **TextFormatRules**.
3. From the **Elements** panel, insert **AllContextsRule**.

4. To specify paragraph formatting, rather than text-range formatting, insert a **ParagraphFormatting** element.
5. Insert **PropertiesBasic**.
6. Insert **ParagraphSpacing**.
7. Insert **SpaceAbove** and type: `10 pt`
8. Click below **SpaceAbove** element, on line descending from **ParagraphSpacing** element.
9. Insert **SpaceBelow** and type: `10 pt`
10. Save your changes.
11. Reimport your element definitions into your test document. If you had errors when importing the element definitions, correct your EDD and reimport.
12. Confirm that the changes you made to the EDD are working as expected.

Formatting cascades in structured documents. Because **Chapter**, the highest level ancestor element in this system is the only place where space above and below are defined, all elements have 10 points of space above and 10 points of space below, until you specify different values on child elements.

## Exercise 3: Specifying an AllContextsRule Referring to Many Properties

In this exercise, you will specify an **AllContextsRule** for the **Title** element that changes the space below to an absolute value of 50 points, makes the text italic, sets the size to 20 points, and sets angle to italic.

You'll also add an autonumber and add a reference frame called **Double Line** under the **Title** element.

To apply the formatting, do this:

1. In the EDD, locate the **Title** element definition.
2. In the **Structure View**, click below the **AttributeList** of the **Title** element.
3. From the **Elements** panel, insert **TextFormatRules**.
4. Insert **AllContextsRule**.
5. Insert **ParagraphFormatting**.
6. Specify **SpaceBelow** of `50 pt`.
   a. Insert **PropertiesBasic**.
   b. Insert **ParagraphSpacing**.
   c. Insert **SpaceBelow** and type: `50 pt`
7. Specify an **Angle** of **Italic** and **Size** of 20 points.
   a. Click below **PropertiesBasic** element, on line descending from the **ParagraphFormatting** element.
   b. Insert **PropertiesFont**.
   c. Insert **Angle**.

      The **Angle** element and an **Italic** child element appear.

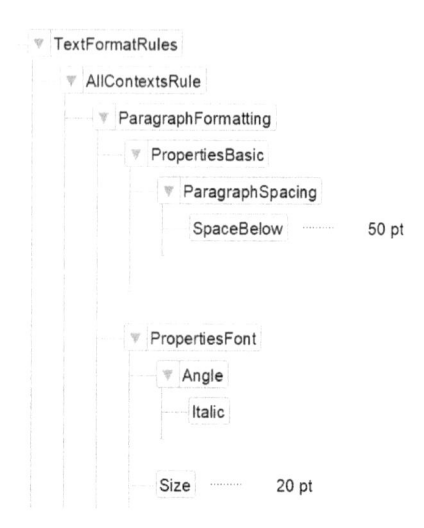

d. Click below the **Angle** element.
   e. Insert **Size** and type: `20 pt`
8. Specify a **Double Line** frame below.
   a. Click below **PropertiesFont** element, on the line descending from the **ParagraphFormatting** element.
   b. Insert **PropertiesAdvanced**.
   c. Insert **FrameBelow** and type: `Double Line`
      **Double Line** is the label of a existing frame on the reference page in your structured template.
9. Specify an **AutonumberFormat** of `C:Chapter <$chapnum>.`
   followed by a space
   a. Click below the **PropertiesAdvanced** element, on the line descending from the **ParagraphFormatting** element.
   b. Insert **PropertiesNumbering**.
   c. Insert **AutonumberFormat** and type: `C:Chapter <$chapnum>.` followed by a space.
10. Save your changes.
11. Reimport your element definitions into your test document. If you had errors when importing the element definitions, correct your EDD and reimport.
12. Confirm that the changes you made to the EDD are working as expected.

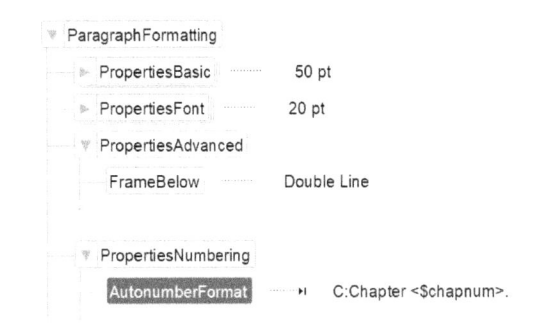

The Title element:
- Has 50 points below
- Is italic with a font size of 20 points
- Has an autonumber displaying as "Chapter 1. "
- Has a double line below

## Exercise 4: Specifying an AllContextsRule Referring to a FormatChangeList

In this exercise, you will specify an **AllContextsRule** for the **Head** element, that refers to a **FormatChangeList** called **HeadTitleText**

To do this:
1. In the EDD, locate the **Head** element definition.
2. In the **Structure View**, click below the **AttributeList** for the **Head** element.

3. From the **Elements** panel, insert **TextFormatRules**.
4. Insert **AllContextsRule**.
5. Insert **ParagraphFormatting**.
6. Insert **FormatChangeListTag**.
7. In **FormatChangeListTag** element, type: `HeadTitleText`
8. Save your changes.

## Exercise 5: Defining a FormatChangeList

In this exercise, you will define the **FormatChangeList** called **HeadTitleText** with a **Weight** of **Bold** and **SpaceAboveChange** of 5 pt.

Elements referencing this list of format changes will be bold, with an additional 5 points of space above them, added to whatever space they have already inherited.

To do this:

1. In the EDD, place your cursor at the end of the **ElementCatalog** element.

   For ease of use, it is often best to define **FormatChangeList** elements at the end of the EDD, below all **Element** definitions.

2. From the **Elements** panel, insert **FormatChangeList**.

   A **FormatChangeList** element and **Tag** child element appear.

3. In the **Tag** element, type: `HeadTitleText`
4. Specify a **Weight** of **Bold**.
   a. Click below **Tag** element, on line descending from **FormatChangeList** element.
   b. Insert **PropertiesFont**.
   c. Insert **Weight**.
   d. Insert **Bold**.
5. Specify a **SpaceAboveChange** of `+5 pt`.
   a. Click below **PropertiesFont** element, on line descending from **FormatChangeList** element.
   b. Insert **PropertiesBasic**.
   c. Insert **ParagraphSpacing**.
   d. Insert **SpaceAboveChange** and type: `+5 pt`
6. Save your changes.
7. Reimport your element definitions into your test document. If you had errors when importing the element definitions, correct your EDD and reimport.
8. Confirm that the changes you made to the EDD are working as expected.

The **Head** element is now bold and has an additional 5 points of space above, for a total of 15 pt.

## Exercise 6: Specifying a Second AllContextsRule

In this exercise, you will specify a second **AllContextsRule** for the **Title** element. The second rule will refer to the **FormatChangeList**, making the text bold and applying the 5 points of space above the element that you defined in the last exercise.

A **FormatChangeList** applies only the formatting properties applicable to the particular context. Because the **Title** element is the first element containing text in the entire structure, **Title** is at the top of the text column. White space above a paragraph at the top of a text column is ignored. Therefore, the **FormatChangeList** will only apply bold, not any additional space to the **Title** element.

1. In the EDD, locate the **Title** element definition.
2. In the **Structure View**, click below the **AllContextsRule** for the **Title** element, on the line descending from **TextFormatRules**.
3. Refer to the **FormatChangeList** tagged **HeadTitleText**.
    a. Insert an **AllContextsRule** element
    b. Insert a **ParagraphFormatting** element
    c. Insert a **FormatChangeListTag** element
    d. In FormatChangeListTag element, type: `HeadTitleText`
4. Save your changes.
5. Reimport your element definitions into your test document. If you had errors when importing the element definitions, correct your EDD and reimport.
6. Confirm that the changes you made to the EDD are working as expected.

The **Title** element is now bold, but does not have an additional 5 points of space above, because it falls at the top of the text column.

## Exercise 7: Specifying an AllContextsRule Referring to Text-Range Properties

In this exercise, you will specify an **AllContextsRule** for the **Term** element, identifying it as a text range with a font change of italics.

Defining **Term** in the EDD as a text range will allow it to be embedded within a paragraph-type element without breaking the text into two paragraphs.

To do this:

1. In the EDD, locate the **Term** element definition.
2. In the **Structure View**, click below the **GeneralRule** of the **Term** element.
3. From the **Elements** panel, insert **TextFormatRules**.

4. Insert **AllContextsRule**.

   An **AllContextsRule** element appears.

5. To specify text-range formatting, rather than paragraph formatting, insert a **TextRangeFormatting** element.

   A **TextRangeFormatting** element and **TextRange** child element appear.

6. Specify an **Angle** of **Italic**.

   a. Insert **PropertiesFont**.

   b. Insert **Angle**.

   An **Angle** element and **Italic** child element appear.

7. Save your changes.

8. If needed, add a **Term** element to your test doc.

9. Reimport your element definitions into your test document. If you had errors when importing the element definitions, correct your EDD and reimport.

10. Confirm that the changes you made to the EDD are working as expected.

The **Term** element is now italic, and no longer causes a break when inserted in a paragraph

[Para for a [*Term*] element]

## Exercise 8: Formatting Captions with Two Rules

In this exercise, you will format the **Caption** for the **Graphic** (both children of **Figure**) by specifying **AllContextsRules** to refer to a **FormatChangeList** and to an autonumbering string.

To do this:

1. In the EDD, locate the **Caption** element definition.

2. In the **Structure View**, click below **GeneralRule** for the **Caption** element.

3. Insert **TextFormatRules**.

4. Attempt the rest on your own, referring to the picture.

5. Save your changes.

6. Reimport your element definitions into your test document. If you had errors when importing the element definitions, correct your EDD and reimport.

7. Confirm that the changes you made to the EDD are working as expected.

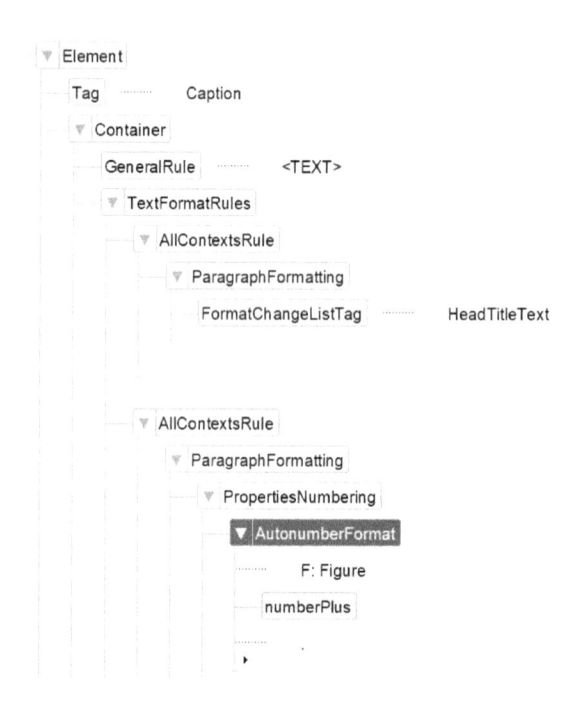

The Caption element is now bold, and has an additional 5 points of space above, for a total of 15 pt. It also has an autonumber prefix displaying as "Figure 1."

Figure 1. [[Figure Caption text]]]

### Exercise 9:   Formatting TableTitle Text

Tables do not inherit their formatting from their ancestors. Table parts inherit formatting from their ancestor table parts, up to the **Table** element. For example, formatting specified for a:

- **Table** element passes to all descendants of the **Table** element
- **TableTitle** element passes to text and children of **TableTitle**
- **TableHeading** element passes to **TableRow** elements in the **TableHeading** and any **TableCells** in the **TableRows** of **TableHeading** only
- **TableBody** element passes to **TableRow** elements in the **TableBody** and any **TableCells** in the **TableRows** of **TableBody** only
- **TableFooting** element passes to **TableRow** elements in the **TableFooting** and any **TableCells** in the **TableRows** of **TableFooting** only
- **TableRow** element passes to its **TableCell** elements
- **TableCell** element passes to text and children of **TableCell**

Without format rules, text in the table is formatted according to the properties of the table format specified in its **InitialTableFormat** (or by any other table format the user chooses from the **Insert Table** dialog upon inserting the **Table** element). Table formats have default paragraph formats defined for use in the table title and cells of the table: **TableTitle, CellHeading, CellBody, CellFooting**. In this exercise, you will format the **TableTitle** for the **Table** with one **AllContextsRule** specifying left alignment and autonumbering of `T:Table <n+>.` (followed by a space).

To do this:

1. In the EDD, locate the `TableTitle` element definition.
2. In the **Structure View,** click below the **GeneralRule** of the **TableTitle** element.
3. Insert **TextFormatRules**.
4. Attempt the rest on your own, referring to the picture.
5. Save your changes.
6. If needed, insert a table into your test document.
7. Reimport your element definitions into your test document. If you had errors when importing the element definitions, correct your EDD and reimport.
8. Confirm that the changes you made to the EDD are working as expected.

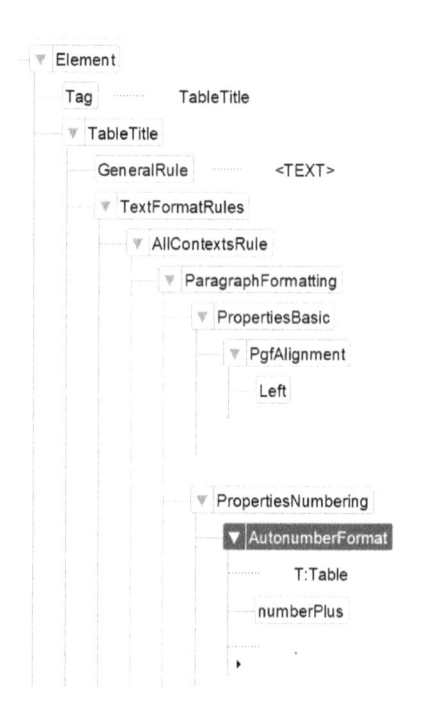

```
▼ Element
    Tag ········· TableTitle
    ▼ TableTitle
        GeneralRule ········· <TEXT>
        ▼ TextFormatRules
            ▼ AllContextsRule
                ▼ ParagraphFormatting
                    ▼ PropertiesBasic
                        ▼ PgfAlignment
                            Left

                    ▼ PropertiesNumbering
                        ▼ AutonumberFormat
                            T:Table
                            numberPlus
                            ▸
```

The **TableTitle** element is now left-aligned, with an autonumber displaying as "**Table 1.**"

**Table 1. Table Title**

|  |  |
|---|---|
|  |  |
|  |  |

# Chapter 11: ContextRule formatting rules

## Introduction

### Objectives

- Write a **ContextRule** with **If**, **ElseIf**, and **Else** clauses
- Write a **LevelRule** with **If**, **ElseIf**, and **Else** clauses
- Analyze syntax for naming ancestors, siblings and attribute values
- Define sub rules and multiple rules
- Write a **ContextLabel**
- Define a **FormatChangeListLimits**

### Overview

Context rules are an optional part of element definitions for:

- Container
- Table, TableTitle, TableHeading, TableBody, TableFooting, TableRow, TableCell
- Footnote

Context rules identify formatting for text in element:

- Rules for **Table, TableHeading, TableBody, TableFooting, TableRow** specify formatting only for text in descendant **TableTitle** and **TableCell** elements
- Changes are considered overrides
- When user reimports element definitions, user can choose to keep or remove overrides

## Writing a ContextRule

Context rules can define one or more possible contexts, with format for each context. They can have separate clauses for different possibilities:

- **If**—only one
- **ElseIf**—zero or more
- **Else**—zero or one

Each If, ElseIf, and Else clause can refer to:

- Named **ParagraphFormatTag** or **CharacterFormatTag** (if text range) stored in document
- Individual paragraph or text-range formatting properties
- **FormatChangeList**

## ContextRule—Naming Ancestors

### Naming just parent

- If **Item** element is within **List** element (regardless of **List**'s ancestors)

103

Element (Container): Item
    General rule: <TEXT>
    Text format rules
        1.  If context is: List
            Numbering properties
                Autonumber format: \b\t

## Less-than-sign (<) for list of ancestors

- If **Item** is within **List** within **Preface** element (regardless of **Preface**'s ancestors)

    Else if **Item** is within **List** with **Chapter** element (regardless of **Chapter**'s ancestors)

    Element (Container): Item
        General rule: <TEXT>
        Text format rules
            1.  If context is: List < Preface
                Numbering properties
                    Autonumber format: \b\t
                    Character format: bulletsymbol
                Else, if context is: List < Chapter
                Numbering properties
                    Autonumber format: <n+>\t

- If **Section** is within two or more **Section** elements

    Element (Container): Section
        General rule: Head, Para+
        Text format rules
            1.  If context is: Section < Section

## Asterisk (*) for unspecified number of successive ancestors

- If **Section** has parent of **Section** and another ancestor tagged **Section** any number of levels up (grandparent, great-grandparent)

    Element (Container): Section
        General rule: Head, Para+
        Text format rules
            1.  If context is: Section < * < Section

## OR indicators (|) to test specification for any ancestor in group

- If **Item** is within **List** that is within **Preface** or **Chapter**

    Element (Container): Item
        General rule: <TEXT>
        Text format rules
            1.  If context is: List < ( Preface | Chapter )

### Exercise 1: Specifying a ContextRule with One Clause Naming a Parent

In this exercise, you will specify a **ContextRule** for the **Section** element that indents a **Section** (and all its descendants) when nested within a parent **Section**.

Because you are using the "change" and "relative" elements, each nested level of **Section** with be indented .5 inches further than the previous as follows:

- **Section** < **Chapter** not indented
- **Section** < **Section** indented .5 inch
- **Section** < **Section** < **Section** indented 1 inch, etc.

To do this:

1. In the EDD, locate the **Section** element definition.
2. In the **Structure View**, click below **AutoInsertions** for the **Section** element.
3. From the **Elements** panel, insert **TextFormatRules**.
4. Insert **ContextRule**.

    **ContextRule**, **If**, and **Specification** elements appear.

5. In the **Specification** element, type: `Section`
6. Click below **Specification** element.
7. Specify **LeftIndentChange** of .5 in and **FirstIndentRelative** of 0

    a. Insert **ParagraphFormatting**.
    b. Insert **PropertiesBasic**.
    c. Insert **Indents**.
    d. Insert **LeftIndentChange** and type: `+.5 in`
    e. Click below **LeftIndentChange** element.
    f. Insert **FirstIndentRelative** and type: `0`

8. Save your changes.
9. Reimport your element definitions into your test document. If you had errors when importing the element definitions, correct your EDD and reimport.
10. Confirm that the changes you made to the EDD are working as expected.

The **Section** element (and all its descendants) is progressively indented in .5 inch increments.

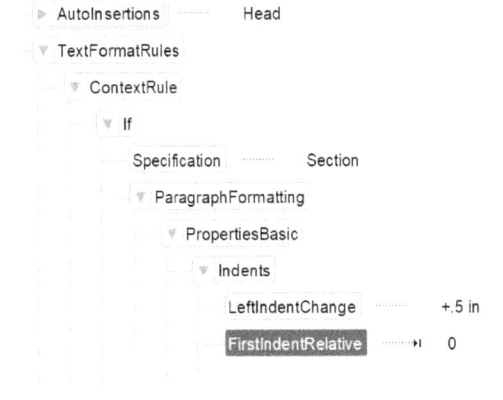

[[Section Head]

[Para text]

    [[Second level section head]

    [Para Text]

        [[Third level section head]

        [Para text]]]

## Exercise 2: Indenting Lists

In this exercise, you will indent your **List** elements (and all their descendants) by specifying a **LeftIndentChange** of .25 inch and **FirstIndentRelative** of zero.

When using the "change" and "relative" elements, indenting of **List** elements will be added to the indenting of **Section** elements as follows:

- **List < Section < Chapter** indented .25 inch
- **List < Section < Section** indented .75 inch
- **List < Section < Section < Section** indented 1.25 inches, etc.

To indent your lists:

1. In the EDD, locate the **List** element definition.
2. In the **Structure View**, click below **AutoInsertions** for the **List** element.
3. From the **Elements** panel, insert **TextFormatRules**.
4. Insert **AllContextsRule**.
5. Specify **LeftIndentChange** of .25 in and **FirstIndentRelative** of 0
   a. Insert **ParagraphFormatting**.
   b. Insert **PropertiesBasic**.
   c. Insert **Indents**.
   d. Insert **LeftIndentChange** and type: `+.25 in`
   e. Click below **LeftIndentChange** element.
   f. Insert **FirstIndentRelative** and type: `0`
6. Save your changes.
7. Reimport your element definitions into your test document. If you had errors when importing the element definitions, correct your EDD and reimport.
8. Confirm that the changes you made to the EDD are working as expected.

   The List element (and all its descendants) is indented in .25 inch more than its parent Section element.

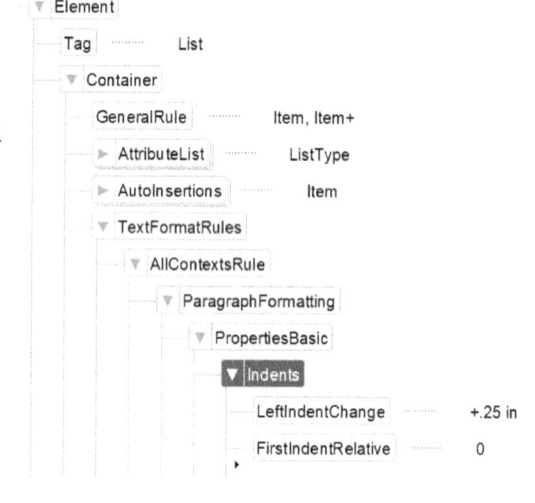

   [Para text]

   [[[Item text]]]

   [[Item text]]]

   [Para text]

## Exercise 3: Specifying a ContextRule with Two Clauses Naming a Parent

In this exercise, you will specify **If** and **Else** clauses for the **WarnNote**, making it bold when a child of **Section** and italic when a child of **Item**.

To specify a context rule that will do this:

1. In the EDD, locate the **WarnNote** element definition.
2. In the **Structure View**, click below **AttributeList** of the **Section** element.

3. From the **Elements** panel, insert **TextFormatRules**.
4. Insert **ContextRule**.

   A **ContextRule**, **If**, and **Specification** element each appear.
5. In **Specification** element, type: `Section`
6. Click below **Specification** element.
7. Specify weight of **Bold**.
   a. Insert **ParagraphFormatting**.
   b. Insert **PropertiesFont**.
   c. Insert **Weight**.
   d. Insert **Bold**.
8. Click below **If** element, on line descending from **ContextRule** element.
9. Insert an **Else** element.
10. Specify **Angle** of **Italic**.
    a. Insert **ParagraphFormatting**.
    b. Insert **PropertiesFont**.
    c. Insert **Angle**.
11. Save your changes.
12. Insert **WarnNote** elements into your test document as needed to test your context rules.
13. Reimport your element definitions into your test document. If you had errors when importing the element definitions, correct your EDD and reimport.
14. Confirm that the changes you made to the EDD are working as expected.

The **WarnNote** element is bold if a child of **Section**, but is otherwise italic

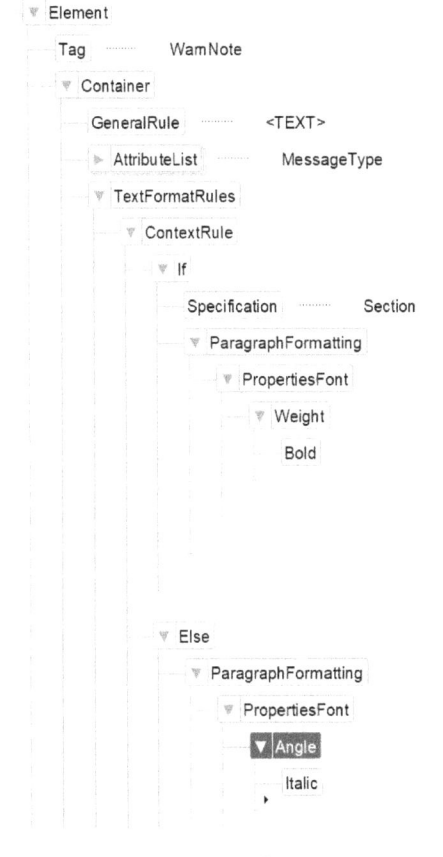

[[Section Head]

[Para for a [*Term*] element]

**[WarnNote as a child of section]**

[Para text]

  [[[Item text]

  *[WarnNote as a child of item]]*

## ContextRule—Naming Siblings and Naming Attribute Values

Sibling indicators describe the relationship of an element to its siblings or an ancestor element to its siblings

| Indicator | Specification is true if element is |
|---|---|
| {first} | First element in its parent |
| {middle} | Neither first element nor last element in its parent |
| {last} | Last element in its parent |
| {notfirst} | Not first element in its parent |
| {notlast} | Not last element in its parent |
| {only} | Only element in its parent |
| {before *sibling*} | Followed by named element or text content |
| {after *sibling*} | Preceded by named element or text content |
| {between *sibling1, sibling2*} | Between named elements or text content |
| {any} | Anywhere in its parent (equivalent to no indicator) |

### An example of the relationship of a current element to its siblings

- If **Item** is first child of its parent **NumberList**

    Element (Container): Item
      General rule: <TEXT>
      Text format rules
        1.  If context is: {first} < NumberList

### An example of the relationship of an ancestor element to its siblings

- If **Head** is child of **Section** which is child of **Chapter**, and only if **Section** immediately follows a sibling **Title**

    Element (Container): Head
      General rule: <TEXT>
      Text format rules
        1.  If context is: Section {after Title} < Chapter

### Attribute indicators describe context based on:

- Attribute name/value pair of current element
- Attribute name/value pair of ancestor element
- Set of attribute name/value pairs
- Operators with attribute name/value pairs

### Attribute name/value pair of current element

- **Note** formatting based on **Label** attribute value

    Element (Container): Note
      General rule: <TEXT>

Attribute list
    1.    Name: Label          Choice          Required
        Choices: Important, Note, Tip

Text format rules
    1.    If context is: [Label = "Important"]
        Default font properties
            Color: Red
        Else, if context is: [Label = "Note"]
        Default font properties
            Weight: Bold
        Else
        Default font properties
            Angle: Italic

## Attribute name/value pair of ancestor element

- If **Item** is within **List** where **Type** attribute of **List** has value of **Bullet**
- Else if **Item** is within **List** where **Type** attribute of **List** has value of **Numbered**

Element (Container): Item
    General rule: <TEXT>
    Text format rules
        1.    If context is: List [Type = "Bullet"]
            Numbering properties
                Autonumber format: \b\t
                Character format: bulletsymbol
        Else, if context is: List [Type = "Numbered"]
            Numbering properties
                Autonumber format: <n+>\t

## Set of name/value pairs, separated with ampersand (&)

- If **Item** is within **List** where Type attribute of **List** has value of **Num** and **Content** attribute has value of **Process**

Element (Container): Item
    General rule: <TEXT>
    Text format rules
        1.    If context is: List [Type="Num" & Content="Process"]

### Operators with attribute name/value pairs

| Operator | With attributes of |
|---|---|
| = (equal to) | All types |
| != (not equal to) | All types |
| > (greater than) | Choice and numeric types |
| < (less than) | Choice and numeric types |
| >= (greater than or equal to) | Choice and numeric types |
| <= (less than or equal to) | Choice and numeric types |

- If **Item** is within **List** where **Type** attribute of **List** does not have a value of **Numbered**

  Element (Container): Item
      General rule: <TEXT>
      Text format rules
          1. If context is: List [Type != "Numbered"]

- Operators with **Choice** attributes evaluates name/value pair using order in list of values in EDD, "lowest value" being one on left

- If **Section** is within **Report** where **Security** attribute of **Report** is any value to the left of **Classified**

  Element (Container): Section
      General rule: Head, Para+
      Text format rules
          1. If context is: Report [Security < "Classified"]

- If **Section** is within **Report** where **Version** attribute **Report** has a value is between 2 and 5, inclusive

  Element (Container): Section
      General rule: Head, Para+
      Text format rules
          1. If context is: Report [Version >= "2" & Version <= "5"]

### Exercise 4: Formatting Paras Using Attribute Values and Sibling Indicators

In your current structure, you can have two types of lists, **Bulleted** and **Numbered**, based of the **ListType** attribute value. List elements contain two or more **Item** elements. **Item** elements contain one or more **Para** elements.

In this exercise, you will specify a rule for the hanging indent and tab position whenever a **Para** is the first child of **Item**, and a rule for the numbering whenever a **Para** is the first child of **Item**.

In a later exercise, you'll simplify this formatting with a **SubRule**, but for now:

1. In the EDD, locate the **Para** element definition.
2. In the **Structure View**, click below the **GeneralRule** of the **Para** element.
3. From the **Elements** panel, insert **TextFormatRules**.
4. Insert **ContextRule**.
   A **ContextRule**, **If**, and **Specification** element all appear.

5. In **Specification** element, type:
   `{first} < Item`
6. Click below **Specification** element.
7. Specify **FirstIndentRelative** of `-.25 in` and **RelativeTabStopPosition** of `0`
   a. Insert **ParagraphFormatting**.
   b. Insert **PropertiesBasic**.
   c. Insert **Indents**.
   d. Insert **FirstIndentRelative** and type: `-.25 in`
   e. Click below **Indents** element.
   f. Insert **TabStops**.
   g. Insert **TabStop**.
   h. Insert **RelativeTabStopPosition** and type: `0`
8. Click below **ContextRule** element.
9. Insert another **ContextRule**.

   **ContextRule**, **If** and **Specification** elements appear.

10. In **Specification** element, type:
    `{first} < Item < List [ListType = "Bulleted"]`
11. Click below **Specification** element.
12. Specify **AutonumberFormat** of `\b\t`
    a. Insert **ParagraphFormatting**.
    b. Insert **PropertiesNumbering**.
    c. Insert **AutonumberFormat**.
    d. Insert **Bullet**.
    e. Insert **Tab**.
13. Click below **If** element.
14. Insert **ElseIf**.

    An **ElseIf** and a **Specification** element appear.

15. In **Specification** element, type:
    `{first} < Item {first} < List [ListType = "Numbered"]`

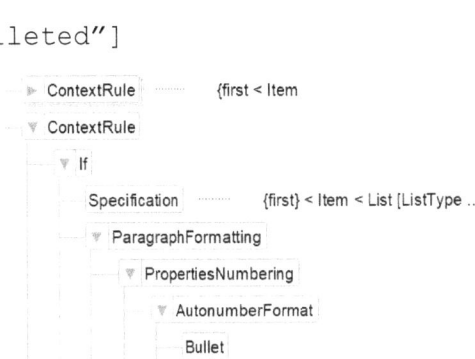

16. Click below **Specification** element.
17. Specify **AutonumberFormat** of `<n=1>.\t`
    a. Insert **ParagraphFormatting**.
    b. Insert **PropertiesNumbering**.
    c. Insert **AutonumberFormat**.
    d. Insert **numberFirst**.
    e. Type a period.
    f. Insert **Tab**.
18. Click below the **ElseIf** element.
19. Insert another **ElseIf** element.

    **ElseIf** and **Specification** elements appear.
20. In Specification element, type:
    `{first} < Item {notfirst} < List [ListType = "Numbered"]`
21. Click below Specification element.
22. Specify **AutonumberFormat** of `<n+>.\t`
    a. Insert **ParagraphFormatting**.
    b. Insert **PropertiesNumbering**.
    c. Insert **AutonumberFormat**.
    d. Insert **numberPlus**.
    e. Type a period.
    f. Insert **Tab**.
23. Save your changes.
24. Reimport your element definitions into your test document. If you had errors when importing the element definitions, correct your EDD and reimport.
25. Confirm that the changes you made to the EDD are working as expected.

.The **Para** element:

- Has a bullet, tab and hanging indent when the first **Para** in any **Item** in a **List** of **ListType Bulleted**
- Displays with "1.", with a tab and hanging indent when the first **Para** in the first **Item** in a **List** of **ListType Numbered**
- Increments the "1." and displays with "2.", "3.", etc., with a tab and hanging indent when the first **Para** in an additional **Item** in a **List** of **ListType Numbered**

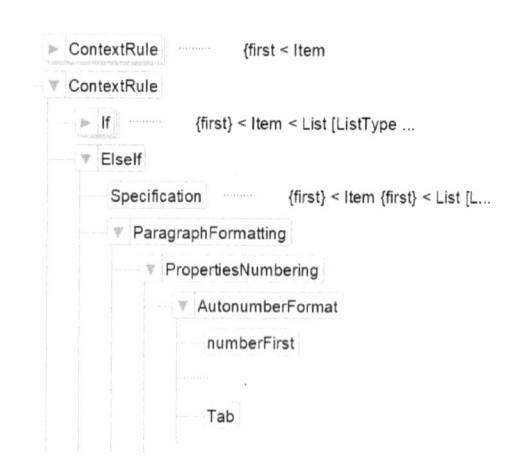

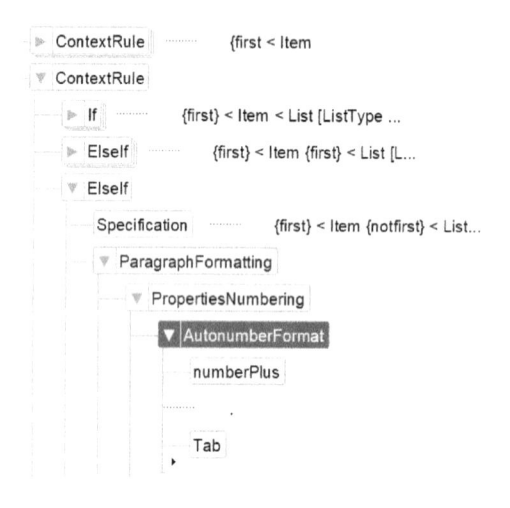

[[Section Head]

[Para before list]

1. [[[Item 1 Numbered]

   [WarnNote (child of Item)]]

2. [[Item 2 Numbered]]]

   [[Section Head]]

   [Para before list]

   - [[[Item 1 bulleted]]

## Exercise 5: Controlling FrameMaker Behavior Using Attribute Values

In this exercise, you will use the attribute value of the **ReadyToImport** attribute on the **Figure** element to determine which dialog (**Import File** or **Anchored Frame**) appears when you insert **Graphic** elements. To do this:

1. In the EDD, locate the **Graphic** element definition.
2. In the **Structure View**, select the **AllContextsRule** element.
3. Delete the **AllContextsRule**.
4. Insert **ContextRule**.

   A **ContextRule**, an **If**, and a **Specification** element appear.

5. In the **Specification** element, type:
   `Figure [ReadyToImport = "Yes"]`
6. Click below **Specification**.
7. Insert **ImportedGraphicFile**.
8. Click below **If**.
9. Insert **Else**.
10. Insert **AnchoredFrame**.
11. Save your changes.
12. Reimport your element definitions into your test document. If you had errors when importing the element definitions, correct your EDD and reimport.
13. Confirm that the changes you made to the EDD are working as expected.

The Graphic element:
- Displays the **Import File** dialog when in a **Figure** with an **ReadyToImport** attribute value of Yes
- Displays the **Anchored Frame** dialog when in a **Figure** with an **ReadyToImport** attribute value of No

# Writing a LevelRule

Level rules define formatting changes that occur when an element is nested within a specified number of levels in an ancestor.

- In a **ContextRule**, **Section < Section < Section** means "nested in at least three Section elements"
- In a **LevelRule**, **Section** count of 3 means "nested in exactly three **Section** elements"
- Can also count instances of current element in hierarchy without specifying the ancestor
- Can have separate clauses for different levels using **If**, **Elself**, and **Else**

Each If, ElseIf, and Else clause specifies formatting changes, referring to:

- Named **ParagraphFormatTag** or **CharacterFormatTag** (if text range) stored in document
- Individual paragraph or text-range properties
- Or **FormatChangeList**

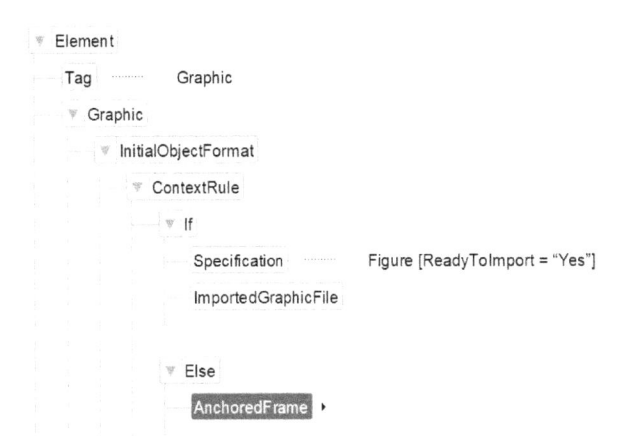

## Exercise 6: Numbering Headings Using LevelRules

In this exercise, you will specify numbering for **Head**, based on nesting level in **Section** ancestors.

1. In the EDD, locate the **Head** element definition.
2. In the **Structure View**, click below **AllContextsRule** for the **Head** element, on the line descending from **TextFormatRules**.
3. Insert **LevelRule**.

   The **LevelRule** element and **CountAncestors** child elements appear.
4. In **CountAncestors** element, type: `Section`
5. Click below **CountAncestors** element.
6. Insert **If**.

   The **If** element and **Specification** child elements appear.
7. In **Specification** element, type: `1`
8. Specify **ParagraphFormatting** of `C:<$chapnum>.<n+>.` followed by a space
   a. Click below **Specification** element
   b. Insert **ParagraphFormatting**
   c. Insert **PropertiesNumbering**
   d. Insert **AutonumberFormat**
   e. Type: `C:<$chapnum>.`
   f. Insert **numberPlus**
   g. Type a period and space
9. Click below **If** element.
10. Insert **Elself**.

    The **Elself** and **Specification** child elements appear.
11. In **Specification** element, type: `2`
12. Specify **ParagraphFormatting** of `C:<$chapnum>.<n>.<n+>.` followed by a space
    a. Click below the **Specification** element.
    b. Insert **ParagraphFormatting**.
    c. Insert **PropertiesNumbering**.
    d. Insert **AutonumberFormat**.
    e. Type: `C:<$chapnum>.`
    f. Insert **number**.
    g. Type a period.
    h. Insert **numberPlus**.
    i. Type a period and space.

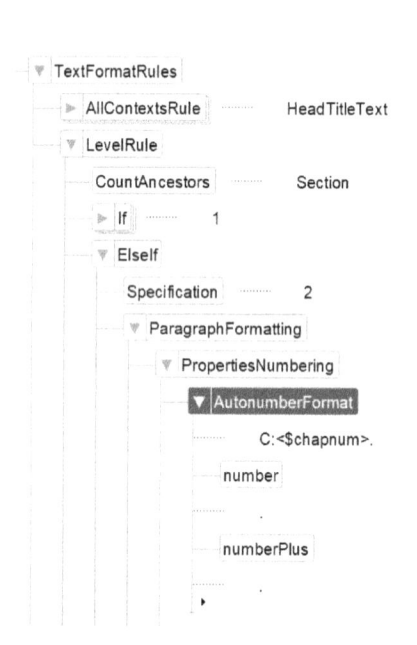

13. Click below **ElseIf** element.
14. Insert another **ElseIf**.

    **ElseIf** element and **Specification** child element appear.
15. In **Specification** element, type: 3
16. Specify **ParagraphFormatting** of
    `C:<$chapnum>.<n>.<n>.<n+>.` followed by a space
    a. Click below **Specification** element.
    b. Insert **ParagraphFormatting**.
    c. Insert **PropertiesNumbering**.
    d. Insert **AutonumberFormat**.
    e. Type: `C:<$chapnum>.`
    f. Insert **number**.
    g. Type a period.
    h. Insert **number**.
    i. Type a period.
    j. Insert **numberPlus**.
    k. Type a period and space.
17. Click below **ElseIf** element.
18. Insert **Else**.

    An **Else** element appears without a **Specification** element.
19. Specify **ParagraphFormatting** of `DO NOT INDENT TO THIS LEVEL` using the color Red.
    a. Insert **ParagraphFormatting**.
    b. Insert **PropertiesNumbering**.
    c. Insert **AutonumberFormat**.
    d. Type: `DO NOT INDENT TO THIS LEVEL`
    e. Click below **PropertiesNumbering**.
    f. Insert **PropertiesFont**.
    g. Insert **Color**.
    h. Type: `Red`
20. Save your changes.
21. Reimport your element definitions into your test document. If you had errors when importing the element definitions, correct your EDD and reimport.
22. Confirm that the changes you made to the EDD are working as expected.

The **Head** element now displays the chapter number, along with the relative nesting of the sections. When nested within more than three **Section** elements, the **Head** element displays an autonumber, in red, of "DO NOT INDENT TO THIS LEVEL".

```
1.1. [[Section Head]]¶
[Para text]¶
    1.1.1. [[Second level section head]]¶
    [Para Text]¶
        1.1.1.1. [[Third level section head]]¶
        [Para text]¶
            DO NOT INDENT TO THIS LEVEL|[Fourth level section head]¶
            [Para text]]]]¶
```

## Using Context Labels

Elements can be assigned context labels in the EDD. Context labels can:

- In some dialogs, allow for a contextual list of element tags for user to select from

    Example: User selects element tags in **Set Up** dialog (**Generate** command) to set up generated file such as index or table of contents

- Distinguish among instances of some elements in these lists

    Example: User might include **Head** elements in table of contents when parent of **Head** is first- or second-level **Section**, but not when parent is more deeply nested **Section**

- Help authors see elements with context labels in dialogs, along with a default group for contexts without a label

Context labels cannot contain white-space characters or any of these special characters:

( ) & | , * + ? < > % [ ] = ! ; : { } "

### Exercise 7: Providing ContextLabels for Headings

In this exercise, you will specifying context labels for **Head**, based on its nesting level in **Section** ancestors.

1. In the EDD, locate the **Head** element definition.
2. In the **Structure View**, click below the **Specification** element for the first **If** clause.
3. From the **Elements** panel, insert a **ContextLabel** element and label it `SectionHead1`
4. In the **Structure View**, click below the Specification element for the first ElseIf clause.
5. From the **Elements** panel, insert a **ContextLabel** element and label it `SectionHead2`
6. In the **Structure View**, click below the Specification element for the second ElseIf clause.
7. From the **Elements** panel, insert a **ContextLabel** element and label it `SectionHead3`
8. Save your changes.

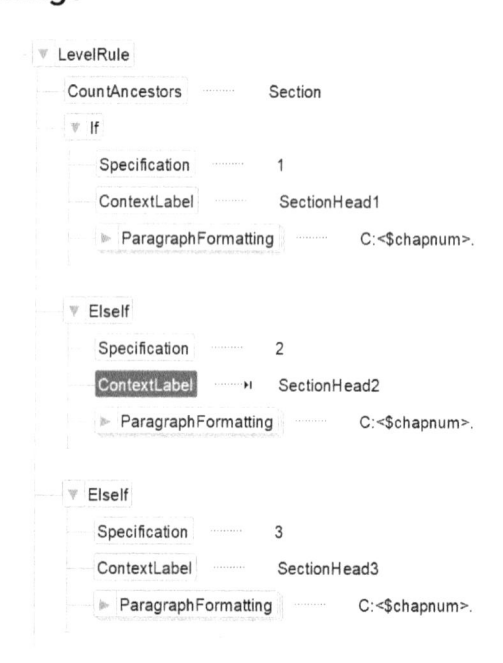

```
▼ LevelRule
    CountAncestors ······ Section
    ▼ If
        Specification ······ 1
        ContextLabel ······ SectionHead1
        ▶ ParagraphFormatting ······ C:<$chapnum>.
    ▼ ElseIf
        Specification ······ 2
        ContextLabel ······▸ SectionHead2
        ▶ ParagraphFormatting ······ C:<$chapnum>.
    ▼ ElseIf
        Specification ······ 3
        ContextLabel ······ SectionHead3
        ▶ ParagraphFormatting ······ C:<$chapnum>.
```

9. Reimport your element definitions into your test document. If you had errors when importing the element definitions, correct your EDD and reimport.

10. Confirm that the changes you made to the EDD are working as expected.

The Head element, when referred to from a dialog, such as the Cross-Reference dialog shown below, uses the following context labels to identify one level of Head from another level:

- SectionHead1 for Head elements nested within exactly one Section element
- SectionHead2 for Head elements nested within exactly two Section elements
- SectionHead3 for Head elements nested within exactly three Section elements
- Otherwise, no label

## Optional Exercise

### Exercise 8: Writing a SubRule for Paras in Items in Lists

In this exercise, you will revise the **TextFormatRules** for a **Para** in an **Item** in a **List** of **ListType** of **Numbered** by replacing two **Elself** clauses with an **Elself** clause containing a **SubRule**.

1. In the EDD, locate the **Para** element definition.

2. In the **Structure View**, select the two **Elself** elements in the second **ContextRule** element.

3. Delete these two **Elself** elements.

4. Rewrite the formatting rules, using one **Elself** with a **SubRule**, referring to this picture, and the Structure View on the following page.

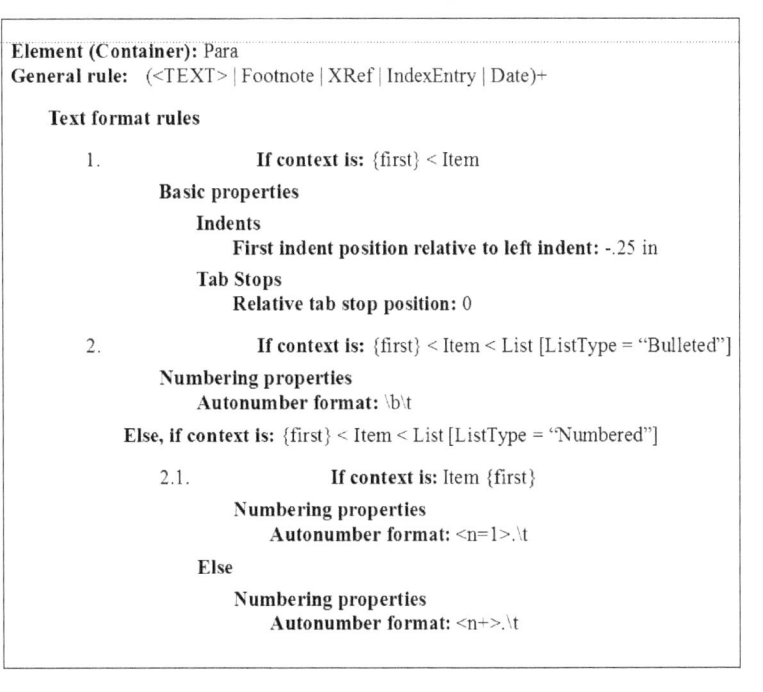

```
Element (Container): Para
General rule:  (<TEXT> | Footnote | XRef | IndexEntry | Date)+

Text format rules
    1.              If context is: {first} < Item
        Basic properties
            Indents
                First indent position relative to left indent: -.25 in
            Tab Stops
                Relative tab stop position: 0
    2.              If context is: {first} < Item < List [ListType = "Bulleted"]
        Numbering properties
            Autonumber format: \b\t
    Else, if context is: {first} < Item < List [ListType = "Numbered"]
        2.1.            If context is: Item {first}
            Numbering properties
                Autonumber format: <n=1>.\t
        Else
            Numbering properties
                Autonumber format: <n+>.\t
```

117

5. Save your changes.

6. Reimport your element definitions into your test document. If you had errors when importing the element definitions, correct your EDD and reimport.

7. Confirm that the changes you made to the EDD are working as expected.

```
▼ TextFormatRules
    ▶ ContextRule         {first} < Item
    ▼ ContextRule
        ▶ If              {first} < Item < List [ListType ...
        ▼ ElseIf
            Specification    {first} < Item < List [ListTyp
            ▼ SubRule
                ▼ ContextRule
                    ▼ If
                        Specification    Item{first}
                        ▼ ParagraphFormatting
                            ▼ PropertiesNumbering
                                ▼ AutonumberFormat
                                    numberFirst
                                    
                                    Tab
                    ▶
        ▼ Else
            ▼ ParagraphFormatting
                ▼ PropertiesNumbering
                    ▼ AutonumberFormat
                        numberPlus
                        
                        Tab
```

The **Para** element is formatted exactly as before, but using a different strategy of writing the formatting specifications:

- Has a bullet, tab and hanging indent when the first **Para** in any **Item** in a **List** of **ListType=Bulleted**
- Displays with "1.", with a tab and hanging indent when the first **Para** in the first **Item** in a **List** of **ListType=Numbered**
- Increments the "1." and displays with "2.", "3.", etc., with a tab and hanging indent when the first **Para** in an additional **Item** in a **List** of **ListType=Numbered**

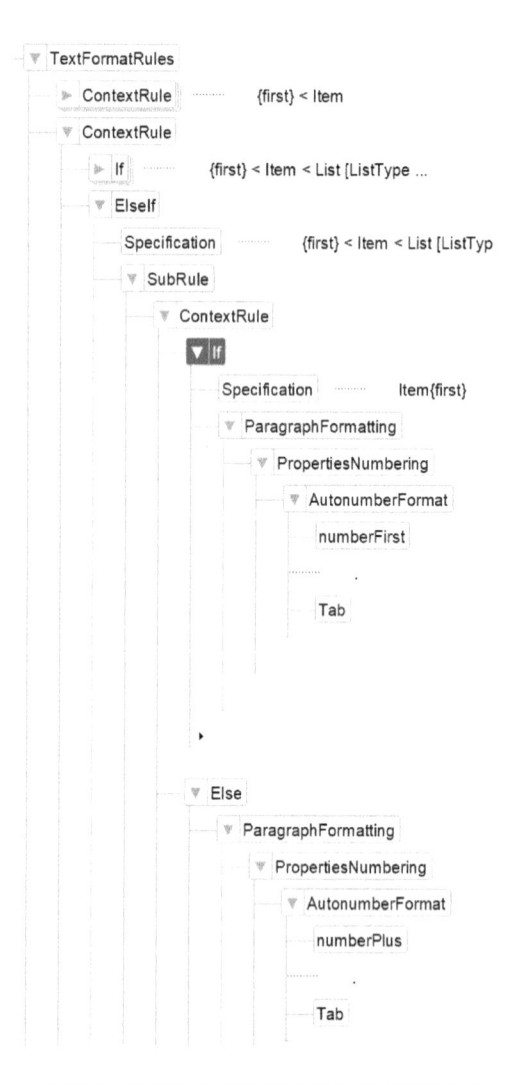

### Chapter 1. Chapter Title

**1.1. Section Head**

Para text

- Item bulleted

    Second Para in item

- Item bulleted

    Second Para in item

Para text

1. Item numbered

    Second Para in item

2. Item numbered

    Second Para in item

# Chapter 12: First/LastParagraphRules

## Introduction

This chapter focuses on the formatting rules for first and last paragraphs in an element.

### Objectives

- Specify **FirstParagraphRules** for formatting
- Specify **LastParagraphRules** for formatting
- Review difference between using **First/LastParagraphRules** and specifying {first}/{last} sibling indicators

### Overview

First/last rules are an optional part of element definitions for **Container** elements only

- They apply a special set of format rules to first or last paragraph in an element
- They are ignored when first/last child element is formatted as a text range
- If an element has prefix formatted in separate paragraph, prefix is first paragraph
- If an element has suffix formatted in separate paragraph, suffix is last paragraph

You can specify First/LastParagraphRules with:

- AllContextsRule
- ContextRule
- LevelRule

## Specifying First/LastParagraphRules

### Exercise 1: Specifying Formatting Properties with First/Last Rules

In this exercise, you will specify that the last paragraph in a **List** element will have extra space below it, regardless if that paragraph is in a **WarnNote**, **Para**, or other element.

1. If it is not already open, from your class files directory, open `EDD.fm`, the EDD you'll be modifying throughout the class.

   If you did not finish the previous chapter's modifications to the EDD, please open **Chapter 12-start First Last Paras.fm** instead, and save it in your class files directory as `EDD.fm`.

For instructions on downloading class files, see "Downloading class files" on page 1.

2. In the EDD, locate the **List** element definition.
3. In the **Structure View**, click below the **TextFormatRules** element.
4. From the **Elements** panel, insert **LastParagraphRules**.
5. Insert **AllContextsRule**.
6. Insert **ParagraphFormatting**.
7. Insert **PropertiesBasic**.
8. Insert **ParagraphSpacing**.
9. Insert **SpaceBelow**.
10. In the **SpaceBelow** element, type: `15 pt`
11. Save your changes.
12. Reimport your element definitions into your test document. If you had errors when importing the element definitions, correct your EDD and reimport.
13. Confirm that the changes you made to the EDD are working as expected.

    The last paragraph in the **List** element, regardless if it is a descendant **Para** or **WarnNote**, has 15 points of space below.

    If you had specified **TextFormatRules** of **SpaceBelow** 15 points for the **List** element, rather than **LastParagraphRules**, each descendant **Item** and their children would have 15 points below, unless you wrote another rule counteracting that inheritance.

    If you had used {last} sibling indicators, you would have had to define the {last} sibling indicators for all potential last children.

```
▼ Element
   Tag ········ List
   ▼ Container
      GeneralRule ········ Item, Item+
      ▶ AttributeList ········ ListType
      ▶ AutoInsertions ········ Item
      ▶ TextFormatRules ········ +.25 in
      ▼ LastParagraphRules
         ▼ AllContextsRule
            ▼ ParagraphFormatting
               ▼ PropertiesBasic
                  ▼ ParagraphSpacing
                     SpaceBelow ········ 15 pt
```

**1.1. Section Head**

Para before list

- Item 1 bulleted
- Item 1 bulleted

Para below List

# Chapter 13: PrefixRules and SuffixRules

## Introduction

This chapter focuses on defining the **PrefixRules** and **SuffixRules** for **Container** elements.

## Objectives

- Define prefix and suffix
- Specify **PrefixRules** and **SuffixRules** using fixed text string
- Specify **PrefixRules** and **SuffixRules** referring to attribute values
- Specify formatting for prefix and suffix
- Compare use of autonumbers, **Prefix/SuffixRules**, and **First/LastParagraphRules**

## Overview

Prefix and suffix are an optional part of element definitions for **Container** elements only

- A prefix is text range defined in EDD that appears at beginning of element (before element's content)
- A suffix is text range defined in EDD that appears at end of element (after content)
- **PrefixRules** and **SuffixRules** describe both text string and any special font properties
- Format rules for prefix/suffix describe font changes only for prefix/suffix
  Font changes do not apply to descendants
- If element has **FirstParagraphRules** and **LastParagraphRules** and prefix/suffix is formatted in a paragraph of its own, prefix/suffix is first/last paragraph for formatting
- Because **PrefixRules** and **SuffixRules** applied after first/last rules, **PrefixRules** and **SuffixRules** can override font changes in first/last rule

## Examples:

### Prefix/suffix for text range element inside a paragraph

- Result: Display double quotation marks around the text of a quotation

    Element (Container): Quotation
        General rule: &lt;TEXT&gt;
        Text format rules
            1.    In all contexts.
                  Text range.
        Prefix rules
            1.    In all contexts.
                  Prefix: "
        Suffix rules
            1.    In all contexts.
                  Suffix: "

### Prefix/suffix for a paragraph, similar to autonumber

- Result: Display **Important:** at beginning of paragraph

    Element (Container): Note
        General rule: &lt;TEXT&gt;
        Prefix rules
            1.    In all contexts.
                  Prefix: Important:

### Prefix/suffix for element with sequence of paragraphs

- Result: Display bold string **Synopsis and Contents**, **Arguments**, or **Examples** in paragraph by itself above First child Para

    Element (Container): Syntax
        General rule: Para+
        Prefix rules
            1.    If context is: Synopsis
                  Prefix: Synopsis and Contents
                Else, if context is: Args
                  Prefix: Arguments
                Else, if context is: Examples
                  Prefix: Examples
            2.    In all contexts.
                Text range.
                Font properties
                      Weight: Bold
        Format rules for first paragraph in element
            1.    In all contexts
                Basic properties
                      Paragraph spacing
                          Space below: 4pt

Format rules for first paragraph puts 4 points of space below the prefix paragraph

### Prefix/suffix for both text range and paragraph

- Result: Display **AuthorNote** element within **Para** as text range, else as paragraph, with prefix/suffix

   Element (Container): AuthorNote
       General rule: <TEXT>
       Text format rules
           1.    If context is: Para
                 Text range.
                     Font properties
                         Angle: Italic
               Else
                   Default font properties
                         Angle: Italic
       Prefix rules
           1.    In all contexts.
                 Prefix: [Author's comments:
                 Text range.
                     Font properties
                         Weight: Bold
       Suffix rules
           1.    In all contexts.
                 Suffix: ]
                 Text range.
                     Font properties
                         Weight: Bold

### Using attribute values in PrefixRules and SuffixRules

- Result: Display value of **Security** attribute in current element

   Prefix: <$attribute[Security]>

- Result: Display value of **Security** attribute in closest ancestor **Item** or **LabelPara**

   Prefix: <$attribute[Security: Item, LabelPara]>

- Result: Display value of **Security** attribute in closest ancestor **Head** element with **Chapter Level** context label

   Prefix: <$attribute[Security: Head(Chapter Level)]>

# Specifying PrefixRules and SuffixRules

### Exercise 1: Specifying Prefix Based on Attribute Value

In this exercise, you will use the **WarnNote** element's **MessageType** attribute value as a prefix for the element and apply to it the color **Red**.

1. If it is not already open, from your class files directory, open `EDD.fm`, the EDD you'll be modifying throughout the class.

    If you did not finish the previous chapter's modifications to the EDD, please open **Chapter 13-start Prefix Suffix.fm** instead, and save it in your class files directory as `EDD.fm`.

For instructions on downloading class files, see "Downloading class files" on page 1.

2. In the EDD, locate the **WarnNote** element definition.
3. In the **Structure View**, click below the **TextFormatRules** element.
4. From the **Elements** panel, insert **PrefixRules**.
5. Insert **AllContextsRule**.
6. Insert **Prefix**.
7. Insert **AttributeValue**.
8. In the **AttributeValue** element, type: `MessageType`
9. Click below the **AttributeValue** element.
10. Type a colon (:) followed by a space.
11. Click below the **Prefix** element.
12. Insert **TextRangeFormatting**.
13. Insert **TextRange**.
14. Insert **PropertiesFont**.
15. Insert **Color**.
16. In the **Color** element, type: `Red`
17. Save your changes.
18. Reimport your element definitions into your test document. If you had errors when importing the element definitions, correct your EDD and reimport.
19. Confirm that the changes you made to the EDD are working as expected.

The **WarnNote** element displays a prefix (in red) of:

- "NOTE: " if using **MessageType** attribute value NOTE.
- "WARNING: " if using **MessageType** attribute value WARNING.

Para for a *Term* element

**WARNING: WarnNote with MessageType=WARNING**

Para text

**NOTE: WarnNote with MessageType=NOTE**

Para text

### Exercise 2: Specifying Quotation Marks Around a Text-Range Element

In this exercise, you will and both a **PrefixRule** and a **SuffixRule** to add quotation marks around the **Term** element.

1. In the EDD, locate the **Term** element definition.
2. In the **Structure View**, click below the **TextFormatRules** for the **Term** element.
3. Insert **PrefixRules**.
4. Attempt the rest on your own, referring to the picture below.
5. Save your changes.
6. Reimport your element definitions into your test document. If you had errors when importing the element definitions, correct your EDD and reimport.
7. Confirm that the changes you made to the EDD are working as expected.

The **Term** element has curved quotes around it in the Document View.

Based on your system, you may want to specify straight quotes, or specific curved quote characters with FrameMaker character codes.

```
▼ Element
    Tag          Term
    ▼ Container
        GeneralRule          <TEXT>
        ▶ TextFormatRules    <WHITESPACE>
        ▼ PrefixRules
            ▼ AllContextsRule
                Prefix           "

        ▼ SuffixRules
            ▼ AllContextsRule
                Suffix       ▸    "
```

#### 1.1.2. Section Head

Para for a *"Term"* element

# Chapter 14: Elements for Structuring Books

## Introduction

In this chapter, you will define book-related elements in the EDD, import them into a chapter in a book, generate the book, adding additional chapters, and a table of contents and index.

### Objectives

- Define element for book
- Define elements for generated files within book
- Generate a structured book
- Add files to structured book
- Generate and format a table of contents
- Generate and format an index
- Wrap generated files into elements of structured book

### Overview

In FrameMaker you can use books to:

- Maintain several documents as one larger document
- Generate table of contents, index, list of figures, list of tables for several files at once
- Allow page sides, page numbering, paragraph numbering to continue across files
- Open, save, print and close all files at once
- Enforce consistent structure of all files within book

A structured book has its own:

- Element hierarchy, which display in the **Structure View**
- List of elements, which display in the **Elements** panel

A book's element definitions are defined in same EDD shared by book's chapters

- They define a container element for the book and specify that it is **ValidHighestLevel**
- They define a container element for each structured file within the book and specify **ValidHighestLevel**
- They define a container element for each generated (unstructured) file within the book with a **GeneralRule** of **<TEXT>**

## Defining and Testing Book Elements

### Exercise 1: Defining an Element for the Entire Book

In this exercise, you will define a **Container** element that is **ValidHighestLevel** for the book as a whole.

1. If it is not already open, from your class files directory, open **EDD.fm**, the EDD you'll be modifying throughout the class.

   If you did not finish the previous chapter's modifications to the EDD, please open **Chapter 14-start Book Elements.fm** instead, and save it in your class files directory as `EDD.fm`.

   For instructions on downloading class files, see "Downloading class files" on page 1.

2. In the EDD, click on the line descending from the **ElementCatalog** element, anywhere above the **FormatChangeListLimits** element at the very end.

3. Create a new **Element** and tag it **UserManual**.
   a. From the **Elements** panel, insert an **Element** element.
      An **Element** and a child **Tag** element appear.
   b. In the **Tag** element, type: `UserManual`

4. Define **UserManual** as a **Container** with a **GeneralRule** of
   `TOC, Chapter, Chapter+, IX?`
   a. Click below the **Tag** element.
   b. From the **Elements** panel, insert **Container**.
      The **Container** element and a **GeneralRule** child element appear.
   c. In the **GeneralRule** element, type: `TOC, Chapter, Chapter+, IX?`

5. Define **UserManual** as **ValidHighestLevel**.
   a. Click above or below the **GeneralRule** element, on the line descending from the **Container** element.
   b. From the **Elements** panel, insert **ValidHighestLevel**.
      **ValidHighestLevel** element and **Yes** child element appear.

   ```
   ▼ Element
     ├─ Tag ········· UserManual
     ▼ Container
       ├─ GeneralRule ········ TOC, Chapter, Chapter+, IX?
       ▼ ValidHighestLevel
         └─ Yes
   ```

6. Save your changes.

### Exercise 2: Defining Elements for the Generated Files

In this exercise, you will define **Container** elements for two generated file elements—**TOC** and **IX**.

1. Create a new **Element** and tag it **TOC**.
   a. From the **Elements** panel, insert an **Element** element.
      An **Element** and a child **Tag** element appear.
   b. In the **Tag** element, type: `TOC`

2. Define **TOC** as a **Container** with a **GeneralRule** of <TEXT>
   a. Click below the **Tag** element.
   b. From the **Elements** panel, insert **Container**.
      **Container** element and **GeneralRule** child element appear.
   c. In the **GeneralRule** element, type: `<TEXT>`
3. Create a new **Element** and tag it `IX`.
   a. From the **Elements** panel, insert an **Element** element.
      An **Element** and a child **Tag** element appear.
   b. In the **Tag** element, type: `IX`
4. Define **IX** as a **Container** with a **GeneralRule** of <TEXT>
   a. Click below the **Tag** element.
   b. From the **Elements** panel, insert **Container**.
      **Container** element and **GeneralRule** child element appear.
   c. In the **GeneralRule** element, type: **<TEXT>**
5. Save your changes.

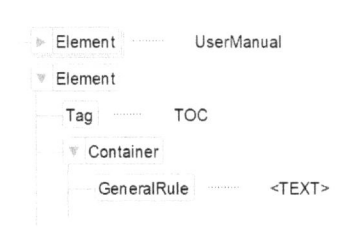

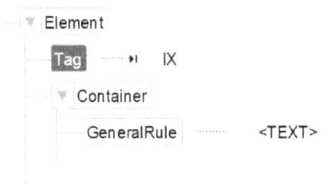

## Exercise 3: Reimporting and Retesting

In this exercise, you will reimport the EDD into the structured template and test your element definitions for **UserManual**, **TOC**, and **IX**.

> Although you will not be using these elements in a single file, it is best to test them in the structured template before importing into the book.

1. Reimport your element definitions into your test document. If you had errors when importing the element definitions, correct your EDD and reimport.
2. Confirm that the changes you made to the EDD are working as expected.
3. In the **Structure View**, select the **Chapter** element (at the top of the structure) and delete it.

   The **Elements** panel displays the UserManual element as valid.
4. Insert a **UserManual** element.

   The **UserManual** is inserted, and the **Elements** panel displays the **TOC** element as valid.
5. Insert **TOC**

   The **Elements** panel displays **<TEXT>** as valid.
6. In the **Structure View**, click below the **TOC** element.

   The **Elements** panel displays the **Chapter** element as valid.

7. Insert **Chapter** then click below it in the **Structure View**.

   The **Elements** panel displays the **Chapter** element as valid again (you have to have two).

8. Insert **Chapter** then click below it in the **Structure View**.

   The **Elements** panel displays the **Chapter** and IX elements as valid.

9. Insert **IX**.

   The **Elements** panel displays **<TEXT>** as valid.

10. Save your changes.

While this structure looks like a book, it isn't as useful as the FrameMaker book structure you may be used to and the numbering isn't acting as we would expect.
In the rest of this lesson you will create a "normal" FrameMaker book with a generated TOC and Index.

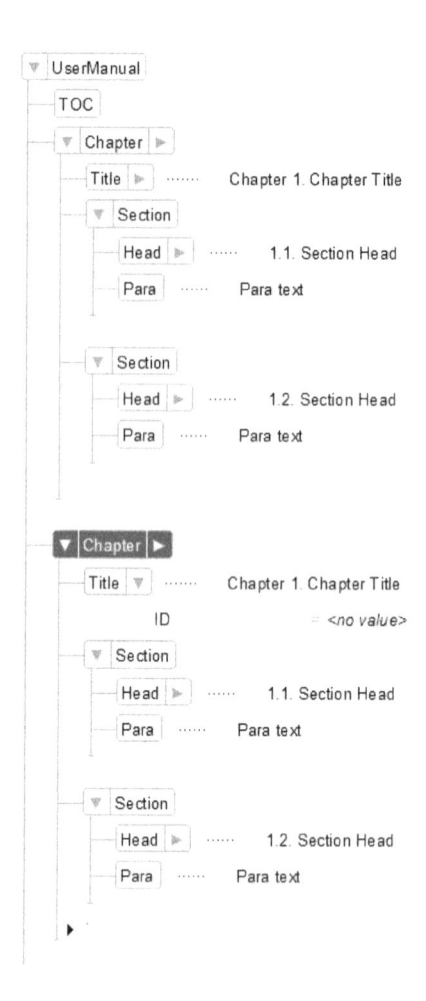

## Generating a FrameMaker Book

### Exercise 4: Importing the Element Definitions into the Chapter

In this exercise, you will import your element definitions into a chapter from which you will then generate the book. The chapter is already structured, using the version of the EDD without the book definitions. Because you are importing into the chapter before generating the book, the book will automatically have the book's element definitions available in its element catalog.

1. From your class files directory, open **chap1.fm**.

   a. From the **File** menu, choose **Open**.

   The **Open** dialog appears.

   b. If necessary, change to your class files directory.

   c. Double-click **chap1.fm**.

   The sample structured document appears. This document already contains the full EDD needed to complete the exercises.

2. Save your changes.

## Exercise 5: Generating a Book

In this exercise, you will create and save a book.

1. With your cursor in the **chap1.fm** file, choose **File > New > Book** menu.

    An alert box appears asking "**Do you want to add the file 'chap1.fm' to the new book?**"

2. Select the **Yes** button to proceed.

    A new book window appears.

    Notice that FrameMaker shows the path of the **chap1.fm** file, but not the path of the book.

    You will save the book to your disk. Afterward, the path of the book will show, and only a relative path to the **chap1.fm** file will remain.

3. With the book window active, choose **File > Save Book As**.

4. If needed, navigate to your class file directory and in the **File name** text box, replace the contents with: `UserManual.book`

    You can manually type in the **.book** extension, but FrameMaker will add it for you if you forget.

5. Click **Save**.

    The book is now saved with its new name. Note the lack of a path for **chap1.fm**, as it is in the same directory as **UserManual.book**.

## Exercise 6: Adding Files

In this exercise, you will add three more chapters to the book.

1. With the book window active, choose **Insert > Files**.

    The **Add Files to Book** dialog appears.

2. Select the **chap2.fm**, **chap3.fm** and **chap4.fm** files.

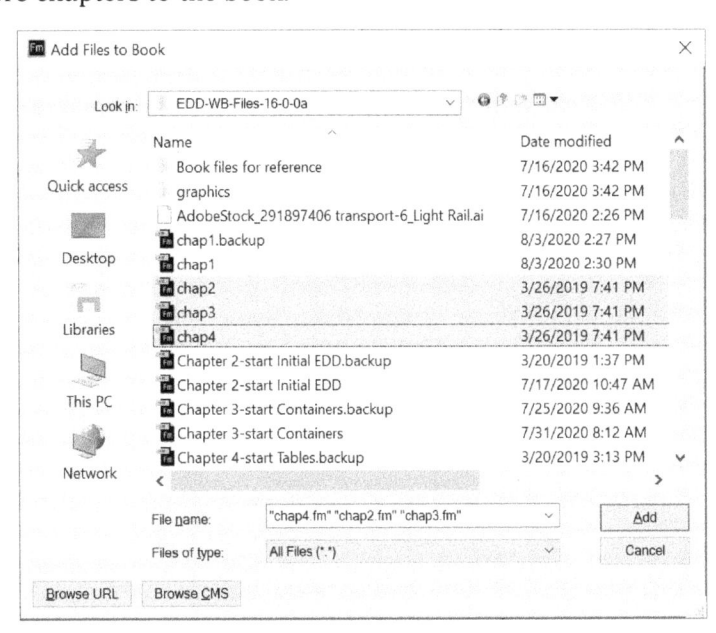

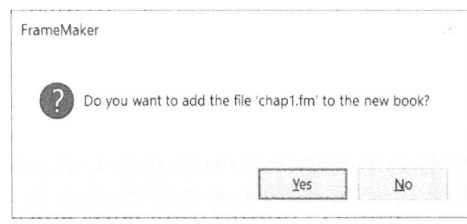

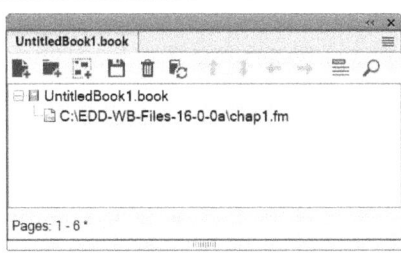

3. Click **Add**.

   The book window updates to display the added files. You'll rearrange the files in the next exercise.

4. With the book window active, from the **File** menu, choose **Save**.

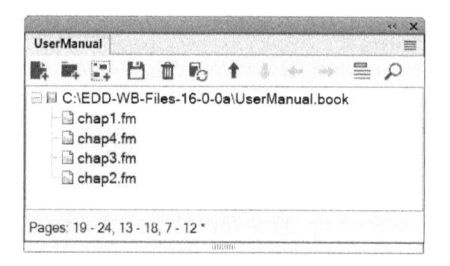

## Exercise 7: Rearranging Files in the Book

In this exercise, you will rearrange the files in the book, putting the four chapters in numerical order. If your chapters are already in numerical order, skip to the next exercise.

1. Rearrange your files as needed by selecting and dragging individual files in either the book window or the structure window.

   You can also move their position by using the arrows above the book name.

2. Move all the files in the book until they are all in the correct order.

3. From the **File** menu, choose **Save**.

The **Structure View** displays the highest-level element as **NoName** and each file as **BOOK-COMPONENT**. You'll correct this in the next exercise.

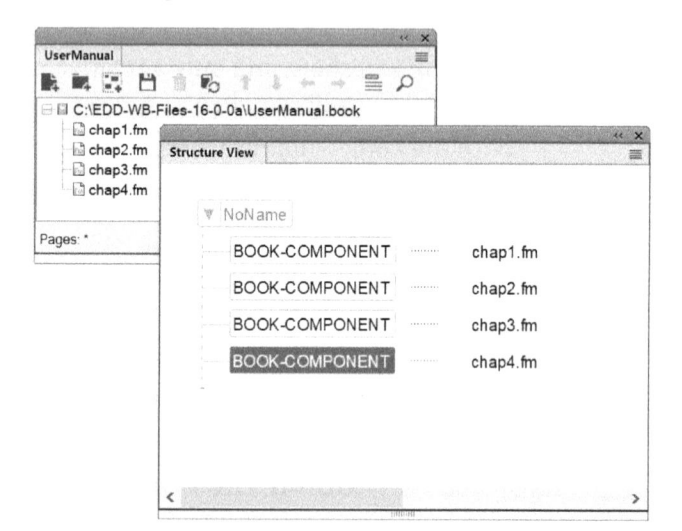

## Exercise 8: Correcting a NoName Element

The **NoName** element at the top of the book window indicates that FrameMaker doesn't yet know what part of the structure should be applied here. In this exercise, you will change the **NoName** element into a **UserManual** element.

1. In the **Structure View**, select the **NoName** element.

2. From the **Elements** panel, select **UserManual** and click **Change**.

   The **Structure View** now shows the highest-level element as **UserManual**, without displaying its label in red.

3. Save your changes.

### Exercise 9: Updating the book to correct Chapter elements in Structure View

In this exercise, you will update the book. Before you update the book, you need to turn off element boundaries in each file. Element boundaries take up space and, therefore, affect the page breaks and page numbering throughout the book and its generated table of contents and index.

In FrameMaker 2015 and earlier, boundaries, text symbols, and other items were managed by individual documents. Starting with FrameMaker 2017, these settings are changed for all open documents. You'll start this exercise by opening all files in book to take advantage of this feature.

1. Ensure that the book window is the active document.
2. Shift+click on the **File** menu, and choose **Open all files in book**. 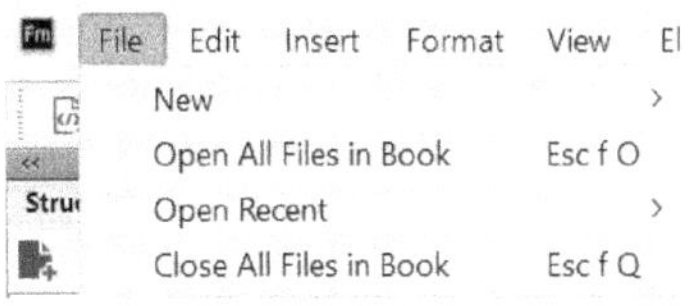
3. From the **View** menu, while a chapter file is the active document, turn off **Element Boundaries**.

    The **Element Boundaries** are now off in all four chapter files.
4. Shift+click the **File** menu again to choose **Save All Open Files** or **Save All Files in Book**.

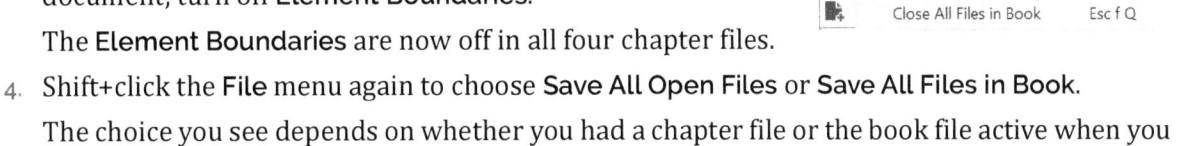

    The choice you see depends on whether you had a chapter file or the book file active when you Shift+clicked the **File** menu.
5. With the book window active, choose **Edit>Update Book**, or use the **Update** button ( ) in the book file.

    The **Update Book** dialog appears.

    Because you have not yet added any placeholders for generated files, nothing appears in the **Generate** and **Don't Generate** fields. 
6. Click **Update**.

    Messages appear at the bottom of the book window showing the progress of the update.

    When done, the **Structure View** displays each file as **Chapter**, the highest-level element in each file. 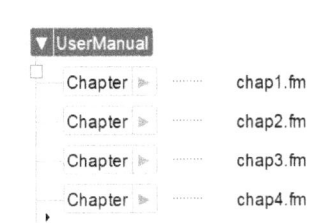
7. With the book window active, shift+click the **File** menu, and choose **Save All Files in Book**.

133

## Exercise 10: Adding a Table of Contents

In this exercise, you will add a table of contents to the book. In the book window, each generated file will have an orange icon to indicate that it is a generated file.

1. In the **Structure View** for your book, position your cursor to the right of the missing content. (to the right of the red square)
2. From the **Insert** menu, choose **Create TOC**.

   The **Setup Table of Contents** dialog appears.

   Because you positioned your cursor above **chap1.fm**, the default settings will place the TOC accurately. Otherwise, you might need to reposition the TOC in the future and regenerate for expected results.

3. Move the following elements to the **Include Elements/Paragraph Formats** scroll list:
   - Head (SectionHead1)
   - Head (SectionHead2)
   - Title

4. Turn on **Create Hypertext Links**.

   Hypertext links will be added to the table of contents, making the TOC clickable in PDF and other formats.

5. Click **OK**.
6. Click **Update**

The **TOC** has been added to the book, but is represented by the BOOK COMPONENT element in the **Structure View**. This unstructured FrameMaker document needs to be wrapped in an appropriate structured element. In this case, you'll need to wrap it in a **TOC** element.

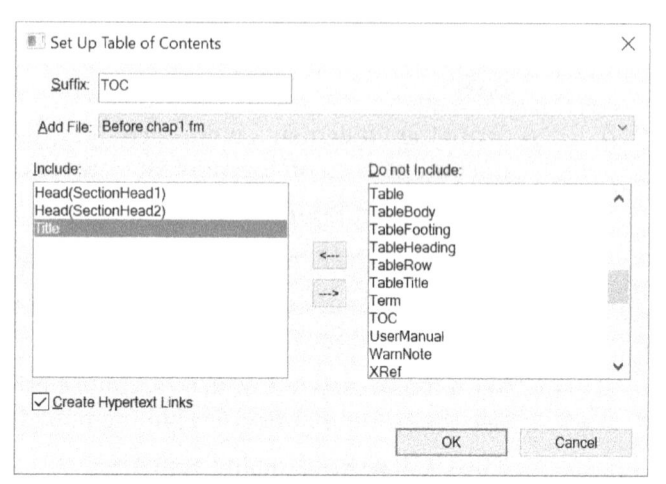

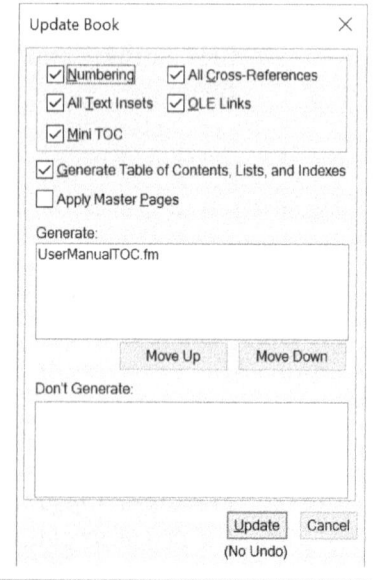

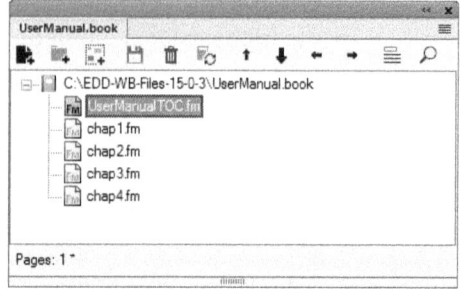

7. Select the **BOOK COMPONENT** in the book file **Structure** View and wrap it in a **TOC** element using the **Elements** panel.

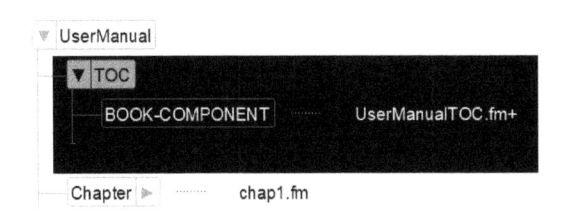

> As of the date of publishing, FrameMaker has a long-standing behavior of opening new generated files like TOC and IX into their own window, rather than opening into the tabbed interface. If this happens to you, just drag the tab of your generated file into the other tabs for your project. You can also use the **Window > Consolidate** command to collect files into the standard tabbed interface. After opening the first time, the files will open as expected.

## Exercise 11: Adding an index

Your sample documents already contain index markers, so you just need to collect them using a generated index file in your book.

1. In the structure window, place your cursor at the end of the book.

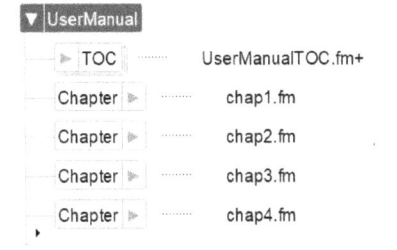

2. Choose **Insert > Standard Index**. Change your settings to match the image, if needed.

3. Click **OK**.

   The **Update Book** dialog appears.

   Make sure that both the **TOC** and **IX** files are in the **Generate** column.

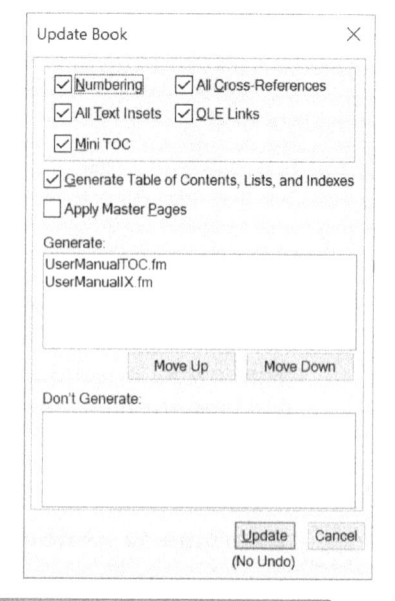

4. Click **Update**.

   The book window updates to display a placeholder for the generated index.

   Notice the difference in color between the generated and non-generated files.

   The **Structure View** displays the index as BOOK-COMPONENT.

   Additionally, the **Structure View** shows a **+** at the end of the generated file filename snippets.

5. With the book window active, from the **File** menu, choose **Save**.

6. Select the **BOOK-COMPONENT** and wrap it in an IX element.

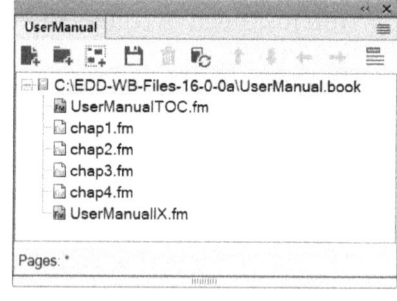

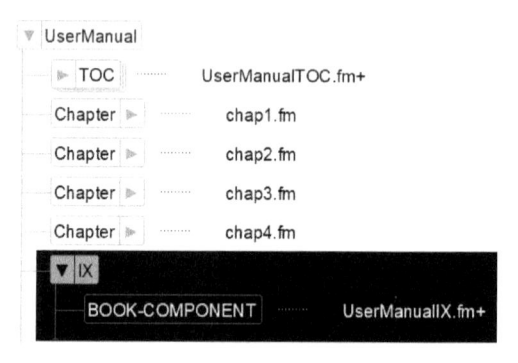

## Exercise 12: Formatting a Table of Contents

In this exercise, you will open a table of contents template and save it with a new name in the book file's directory. This will result in an automatically formatted table of contents when you generate/update the book.

1. From your class files directory, open **toc.tpl.fm**.

   a. From the **File** menu, choose **Open**.

      The **Open** dialog appears.

   b. If necessary, change to your class files directory.

c. Double-click **toc.tpl.fm**.

   The document appears.

2. Choose **File>Save As**, save the file as `UserManualTOC.fm` in your class files directory.

   The table of contents will be populated when you update the book in a later exercise.

> You can also use File>Import>Formats to import the toc.tpl.fm formats into the UserManualTOC.fm file.

3. Close UserManualTOC.fm

> Make sure to close the TOC so that the Update Book exercise later works as expected.

> To learn more about formatting tables of contents, indexes, and other FrameMaker formatting options, see my reference book, *FrameMaker - Working with Content,* or consider taking my template design course. Information on both books and courses is available at www.techcommtools.com.

## Exercise 13: Formatting an Index

In this exercise, you will open an index template and save it with a new name in the book file's directory.

1. From your class files directory, open **ix.tpl.fm**.

   a. From the **File** menu, choose **Open**.

      The **Open** dialog appears.

   b. If necessary, change to your class files directory.

   c. Double-click **ix.tpl.fm**.

      The document appears.

2. Using Save As, save **ix.tpl** as `UserManualIX.fm` in your class files directory.

   The index will be populated when you generate/update the book in the next exercise.

> You can also use File>Import>Formats to import the IX.tpl.fm formats into the UserManualTOC.fm file.

3. Close UserManualIX.fm.

> Make sure to close the TOC so that the Update Book exercise later works as expected.

## Exercise 14: Setting up the Book Files

In this exercise, you will set up the page side, page numbering, paragraph numbering, and prefix for each file in the book.

1. In the book window, right-click on **UserManualTOC.fm** and choose **Numbering**.

   The **Numbering Properties** dialog appears.

2. On the **Page** tab, match the **First Page #** and **Format** options as shown.

3. Click **Set**.

4. In the book window, right-click on **chap1.fm** and choose **Numbering**.

   a. On the **Page** tab, set **First Page** to 1 and format to **Numeric**.

   b. On the **Chapter** tab set the properties as shown.

5. Click **Set**.

6. Select all the files after **chap1.fm** in the book window.

7. Right-click on the selected files and choose **Numbering**.

   a. On the **Chapter** tab, select the **Continue Numbering From Previous Chapter in Book** radio button.

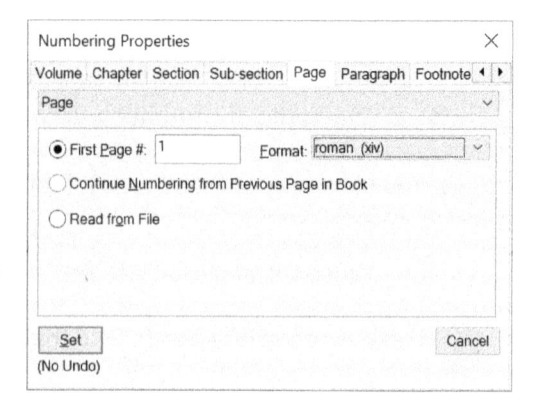

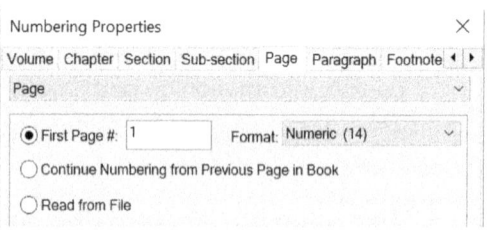

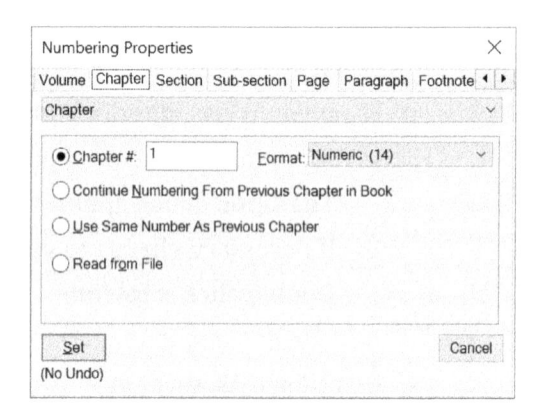

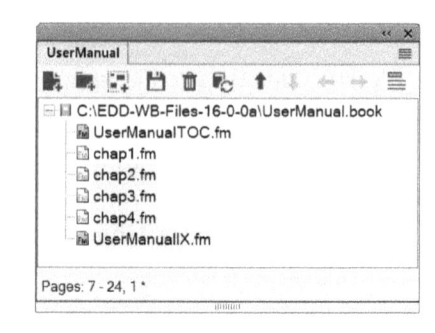

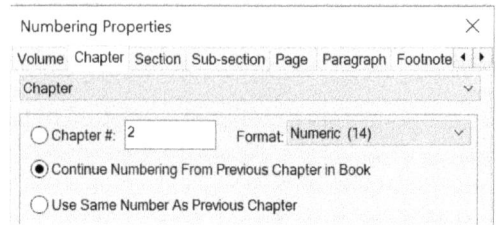

138

b. Move to the **Page** tab and select the **Continue From Previous Page in Book** radio button.
8. Click **Set**.

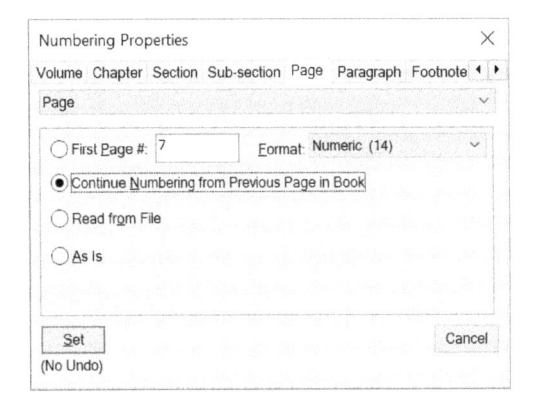

## Exercise 15: Update the Book

In this exercise, you will update the book to fix page sides and numbering and update paragraph numbering and populate the generated files.

1. Select the **Update** button ( ) in the book file.

   The **Update Book** dialog appears.

2. Click **Update**.

   Messages appear at the bottom of the book window showing the progress of the update.

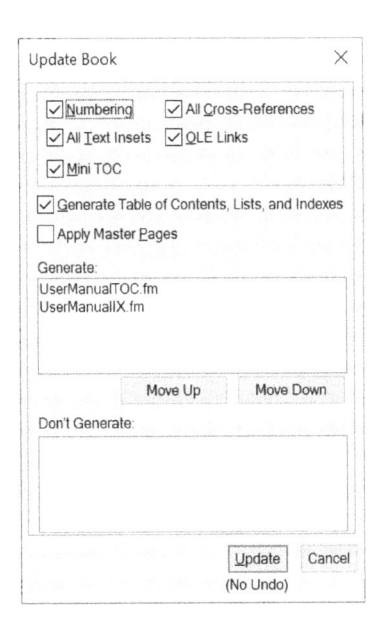

   When done, the **Structure View** continues to display each file as **Chapter**, the highest-level element in each file, except for the generated files which still display as **BOOK-COMPONENT**.

3. With the book window active, shift-click the **File** menu, choose **Save All Files in Book**.

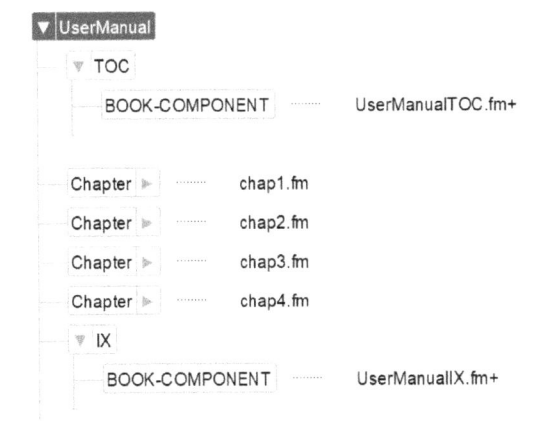

---

If you get a book error log related to inconsistent numbering properties, save all files in book, close the book error log, and update again.

139

## Exercise 16: Reviewing the Book Files

In this exercise, you will open and check the newly generated table of contents and index.

1. From the book window, double-click the table of contents file.

   The table of contents opens, already formatted because you saved the table of contents template with the correct file name.

> If the formats don't appear correctly for either the TOC or IX, you can use **File > Import > Formats** to bring formats in from the corresponding template file.

2. Review the entries in the table of contents.
3. Close the table of contents.
4. From the book window, double-click the index file.

   The index opens, already formatted because you saved the index template with the correct file name.

5. Review the entries in the index.
6. Close the index.
7. From the book window, double-click each chapter, noticing the continuation of the chapter numbering across the files.

# Chapter 15: Structuring Unstructured Data

## Introduction

In this chapter, you will set up a conversion table and define object and element mapping in it. After defining the conversion table, you will use its mapping to add structure to unstructured documents.

### Objectives

- Learn conversion rule syntax
- Generate conversion table
- Learn how to create conversion table from scratch
- Structure a currently unstructured document
- Structure a group of unstructured files
- Structure unstructured book

### Overview

There are two ways to wrap unstructured data

- Method 1—Manually, element by element. This method is only good for very small conversions.
- Method 2—Automatically, using the tools available in **Structured > Utilities**

Automatic wrapping requires a conversion table, which is usually created by application developer. The table:

- Provides mappings to automate the task of adding structure to unstructured documents
- Uses paragraph and character tags, and object types (such as equations or footnotes), to identify how to wrap document components in elements
- Also specifies how to wrap child elements in parent elements

Here is the organization of the conversion table itself:

- A regular table, with at least 3 columns and 1 body row
- It has additional columns and heading/footing rows for comments and labeling
- Each body row holds 1 rule. Here is a breakdown of table organization:

| Column 1 | Column 2 | Column 3 |
|---|---|---|
| specifies document object, child element, or sequence to wrap | specifies element in which to wrap | specifies optional qualifier ("nickname") to use as temporary label |

A conversion table can be split up into several tables with text or graphics in between for comments

- It cannot have any tables other than conversion tables
- The table must be saved before it can be used

## Rule Syntax—Character Restrictions

- Tags are case-sensitive and tags in tables must exactly match tags in docs to be converted.
- Qualifier tags are case-sensitive and two occurrences of one qualifier must match exactly

Qualifiers for these special characters in tags: ( ) & | , * + ? % [ ] : \

- Are allowed in format tags and qualifier tags— but only if preceded by a backslash (\) in the table
- Are not allowed in element tags

A space character in tags does not need to be preceded with a backslash
(For example, the tag **Format A** is valid)

## Wildcard character (%) in Tags:

- Use % as in format or element tag to match zero, one, or more characters (similar to * in general rule)
- For example, P:%Body matches paragraphs with the format tag Body, FirstBody, or BulletBody

## Methods for Producing a Conversion Table

- Method 1—FrameMaker Generates Initial Table (easiest, recommended, and is the method used in this course). Once created, it can be modified as needed by hand.
- Method 2—Create a conversion table from scratch (requires creating and populating entries for all catalog entries, and not recommended)

**Exercise 1: Generating Initial Conversion Table**

In this exercise, you will generate a conversion table from an unstructured document.

1. From your class files directory, open **wraptest.fm**.
    a. From the **File** menu, choose **Open**.
       The **Open** dialog appears.
    b. If necessary, change to your class files directory.
    c. Double-click **wraptest.fm**.

For instructions on downloading class files, see "Downloading class files" on page 1.

The document appears.

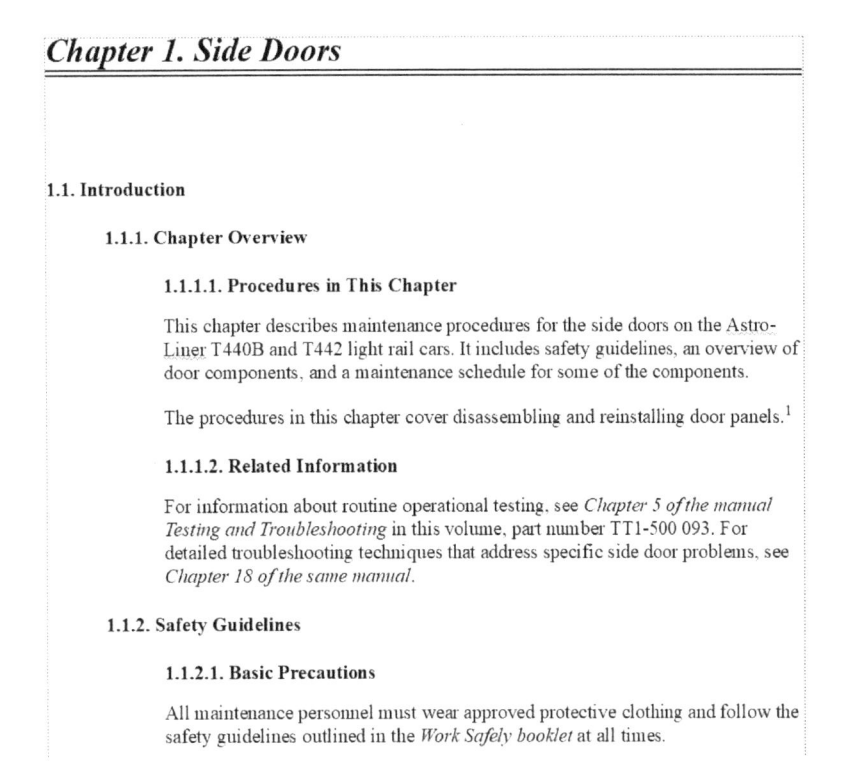

> **Chapter 1. Side Doors**
>
> **1.1. Introduction**
>
> **1.1.1. Chapter Overview**
>
> **1.1.1.1. Procedures in This Chapter**
>
> This chapter describes maintenance procedures for the side doors on the Astro-Liner T440B and T442 light rail cars. It includes safety guidelines, an overview of door components, and a maintenance schedule for some of the components.
>
> The procedures in this chapter cover disassembling and reinstalling door panels.[1]
>
> **1.1.1.2. Related Information**
>
> For information about routine operational testing, see *Chapter 5 of the manual Testing and Troubleshooting* in this volume, part number TT1-500 093. For detailed troubleshooting techniques that address specific side door problems, see *Chapter 18 of the same manual*.
>
> **1.1.2. Safety Guidelines**
>
> **1.1.2.1. Basic Precautions**
>
> All maintenance personnel must wear approved protective clothing and follow the safety guidelines outlined in the *Work Safely booklet* at all times.

2. Open the **Structure View** and **Elements** panels.

   Both the **Structure View** and **Elements** panels are blank because this is an unstructured document.

3. Scroll through the document, clicking in various paragraphs to identify the paragraph formats being used.

4. From the **File** menu, choose **Structure > Utilities > Generate Conversion Table**.

   The **Generate Conversion Table** dialog appears.

5. Select **Generate New Conversion Table** and click **Generate**.

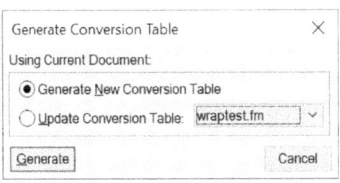

A conversion table, based on your document's format tags, appears.

| Wrap this object or objects | In this element | With this qualifier |
|---|---|---|
| P:Title | Title | |
| P:H1 | H1 | |
| P:H2 | H2 | |
| P:H3 | H3 | |
| P:Regular | Regular | |
| P:Bulleted | Bulleted | |
| P:Caption | Caption | |
| P:TableTitle | TableTitle | |
| P:Pname | Pname | |
| P:Pnum | Pnum | |
| P:Pcount | Pcount | |
| P:Indented | Indented | |
| P:StepFirst | StepFirst | |
| P:Step | Step | |
| P:Note | Note | |
| C:Emphasis | Emphasis | |
| C:WarnNote | WarnNote | |
| X:ElemNumTextPage | ElemNumTextPage | |
| M:Index | Index | |
| M:Cross-Ref | Cross-Ref | |
| G: | GRAPHIC | |
| F:flow | FOOTNOTE | |
| T:Format A | FormatA | |
| TT: | TITLE | |
| TH: | HEADING | |
| TB: | BODY | |
| TF: | FOOTING | |
| TR: | ROW | |
| TC: | CELL | |

6. Use the **Save As** dialog to save this new untitled document into your class files directory with the new filename `Conversion Table.fm`
    a. From the **File** menu, choose **Save As**.
       The **Save Document** dialog appears.
    b. If necessary, change to your class files directory.
    c. In the **Save in File** field, delete the current file name and type: `Conversion Table.fm`
    d. Click **Save**.

# Typing the Conversion Rules

Conventions for Column 1 of the conversion table:

- Type a one- or two-letter code to identify the type of item
- Type a format (optional) to narrow the definition

| For this object | Use this Code | Followed by optional |
|---|---|---|
| Paragraph | P: | Paragraph format tag |
| Text range | C: | Character format tag |
| Table | T: | Table format tag |
| Table title | TT: | (none) |
| Table heading | TH: | (none) |
| Table body | TB: | (none) |
| Table row | TR: | (none) |
| Table cell | TC: | (none) |
| System variable | SV: | Variable format name |
| User variable | UV: | Variable format name |
| Graphic (anchored frame or imported object) | G: | (none) |
| Footnote | F: | Location of footnote: Table or Flow |
| Marker | M: | Marker type |
| Cross-reference | X: | Cross-reference format |
| Text Inset | TI: | (none) |
| Equation | Q: | Size of equation: Small, Medium, or Large |
| Element | E: | Element tag (used to wrap elements in higher-level elements) |

Conventions for Column 2 of the conversion table:
- Type the object identifier **E:** (optional)
- Followed by an element tag

Conventions for Column 3 of the conversion table:
- Type a qualifier (optional) for the new element tag
- Qualifiers are used in later rules to differentiate elements of the same name when wrapping in higher-level elements

Conventions wrapping a sequence of elements, in Column 1:
- Type **E:** for element
- Type an element tag
- Type a qualifier (optional) in brackets
- Add more element tags with code identifiers
- Use these symbols to further describe the sequence

| Symbol | Meaning |
| --- | --- |
| Plus sign (+) | Item is required and can occur more than once |
| Question mark (?) | Item is optional and can occur once |
| Asterisk (*) | Item is optional and can occur more than once |
| Comma (,) | Items must occur in the order given |
| Ampersand (&) | Items can occur in any order |
| Vertical bar (|) | Any one of the items in the sequence can occur |
| Parentheses | Beginning and end of a sequence |

To specify an attribute for an element, in Column 2:
- Type the attribute name and value in brackets after the element tag in the second column of the table
- Separate the name and value with an equal sign, and enclose the value in double quotation marks

If naming a table element from one or more child elements, in Column 1:
- Type the object identifier **TE:**
- Followed by **E:**
- Followed by an element tag
- Type a qualifier (optional) in brackets

To promote anchored objects, in Column 2:
- Type the element tag for the table or graphic
- Add the keyword "**promote**" in parentheses after the element tag for the table or graphic

To flag format overrides, in Column 1:
- Add the rule "flag paragraph format overrides"
- Add the rule "flag character format overrides"

To wrap untagged text:
- In Column 1, add the rule "untagged character formatting"
- In Column 2, add an element tag

## Exercise 2: Writing Rules for Text Ranges

In this exercise, you will modify the existing rules for text ranges to match the element tags in Final EDD.fm.

1. Locate the following rule:

   | Wrap this object or objects | In this element | With this qualifier |
   |---|---|---|
   | C:Emphasis | Emphasis | |

2. Text using character tag **Emphasis** should be wrapped in **WarnNote**. Once wrapped, the **Emphasis** character tag is not necessary, as the **TextFormatRules** for **WarnNote** specify the formatting of **Angle Italic**.

   For this reason, rewrite the rule as follows:

   | | | |
   |---|---|---|
   | C:Emphasis | WarnNote | |

3. Text using character tag **WarnNote** does not need to be wrapped. This text corresponds with the prefix for the **WarnNote** element. This rule is not necessary at all, as the **PrefixRules** for **WarnNote** specify the red color for the prefix.

   For this reason, find and delete this following rule entirely:

   | Wrap this object or objects | In this element | With this qualifier |
   |---|---|---|
   | C:WarnNote | WarnNote | |

4. Save your changes.

## Exercise 3: Writing Rules for Paragraphs

In this exercise, you will modify the existing rules for paragraphs to match the element tags in **Final EDD.fm**.

1. Locate the following rules:

| Wrap this object or objects | In this element | With this qualifier |
|---|---|---|
| P:H1 | H1 | |
| P:H2 | H2 | |
| P:H3 | H3 | |

Text using paragraph tag **H1** should be wrapped in **Head**. To differentiate this **Head** from **Head** elements at other nesting levels, give it a qualifier of **SH1**.

Text using paragraph tag **H2** should be wrapped in **Head**. To differentiate this **Head** from other **Head** elements, give it a qualifier of **SH2**.

Text using paragraph tag **H3** should be wrapped in **Head**. To differentiate this **Head** from other **Head** elements, give it a qualifier of **SH3**.

For these reasons, rewrite these rules as follows:

| | | |
|---|---|---|
| P:H1 | Head | SH1 |
| P:H2 | Head | SH2 |
| P:H3 | Head | SH3 |

2. Locate the following rules:

| Wrap this object or objects | In this element | With this qualifier |
|---|---|---|
| P:Regular | Regular | |
| P:Bulleted | Bulleted | |
| P:Indented | Indented | |
| P:StepFirst | StepFirst | |
| P:Step | Step | |

Text using paragraph tag **Regular** should be wrapped in **Para**. To differentiate this **Para** from **Para** elements within lists, give it a qualifier of **Regular**.

Text using paragraph tag **Bulleted** should be wrapped in **Para**. To differentiate this **Para** which appears within a bulleted list, give it a qualifier of **Bull**.

Text using paragraph tag **Indented** should be wrapped in **Para**. To differentiate this **Para** which serves as a substep to bulleted or numbered items in **List** elements, give it a qualifier of **Substep**.

Text using paragraph tag **StepRestart** should be wrapped in **Para**. To differentiate this **Para** which restarts a numbered list, give it a qualifier of **Step1**.

Text using paragraph tag **Step** should be wrapped in **Para**. To differentiate this **Para** which continues a numbered list, give it a qualifier of **Step**.

For these reasons, rewrite these rules as follows:

| P:Regular | Para | Regular |
|---|---|---|
| P:Bulleted | Para | Bull |
| P:Indented | Para | Substep |
| P:StepFirst | Para | Step1 |
| P:Step | Para | Step |

3. Find the following rule:

| Wrap this object or objects | In this element | With this qualifier |
|---|---|---|
| P:Note | Note | |

Text using paragraph tag **Note** should be wrapped in **WarnNote**.

For this reason, rewrite this rule as follows:

| P:Note | WarnNote | |
|---|---|---|

4. Save your changes.

## Exercise 4: Writing Rules for Footnotes

In this exercise, you will modify the existing rules for footnotes to match the element tags in `Conversion Table.fm`.

1. Locate the following rule:

   | Wrap this object or objects | In this element | With this qualifier |
   |---|---|---|
   | F:flow | FOOTNOTE | |

   Footnotes in the main flow should be wrapped in **Footnote** (initial capital letter only).

   For this reason, rewrite this rule as follows:

   | Wrap this object or objects | In this element | With this qualifier |
   |---|---|---|
   | F:flow | Footnote | |

   Additionally, although you did not have table footnotes in this particular example, you may in other unstructured documents for which you want to use the same conversion table.

   For this reason, add the following rule:

   | Wrap this object or objects | In this element | With this qualifier |
   |---|---|---|
   | F:table | Footnote | |

2. Save your changes.

## Exercise 5: Writing Rules for Cross-References

In this exercise, you will modify the existing rules for cross-references to match the element tags in Final EDD.fm.

1. Locate the following rule:

   | Wrap this object or objects | In this element | With this qualifier |
   |---|---|---|
   | X:ElemNumTextPage | ElemNumTextPage | |

   Cross-references need to be wrapped in **XRef**, so rewrite the rule as follows:

   | Wrap this object or objects | In this element | With this qualifier |
   |---|---|---|
   | X:ElemNumTextPage | XRef | |

2. Save your changes.

## Exercise 6: Writing Rules for Equations

In this exercise, you will create a rule for equations to match the element tags in Final EDD.fm.

1. Add the following rule anywhere in the table (creating a new table row, if necessary):

   | Wrap this object or objects | In this element | With this qualifier |
   |---|---|---|
   | Q: | EQ (promote) | |

   You could specify an equation size of **Small**, **Medium** or **Large**, but you want to wrap all equations in **EQ**, regardless of their size.

Adding the word "(promote)" makes EQ elements a sibling, rather than a child, of the paragraph element in which they are anchored.

2. Save your changes.

## Exercise 7: Writing Rules for Graphics

In this exercise, you will modify the existing rule for graphics to match the element tags in **Final EDD.fm**.

1. Locate the following rule:

| Wrap this object or objects | In this element | With this qualifier |
|---|---|---|
| G: | GRAPHIC | |

Graphics should be wrapped in Graphic (initial capital letter only). Adding the word "(promote)" makes them a sibling, rather than a child, of the paragraph element in which they are anchored. According to the EDD, they should be a sibling of **Caption**, not a child.

For this reason, rewrite this rule as follows:

| | | |
|---|---|---|
| G: | Graphic (promote) | |

2. Save your changes.

## Exercise 8: Writing Rules for Markers

In this exercise, you will modify the existing rule for index markers and delete the rule for cross-reference markers to match the element tags in **Final EDD.fm**.

1. Locate the following rules:

| Wrap this object or objects | In this element | With this qualifier |
|---|---|---|
| M:Index | Index | |
| M:Cross-Ref | Cross-Ref | |

Cross-Ref markers should not be wrapped. You will be using element-based cross-referencing based on attributes, so delete the second rule entirely.

2. Index markers should be wrapped in an **IndexEntry** element, so rewrite the Index rule as follows:

| | | |
|---|---|---|
| M:Index | IndexEntry | |

3. Save your changes.

## Exercise 9: Writing Rules for Tables and Table Parts

In this exercise, you will modify the existing rules for tables and table parts to match the element tags in **Final EDD.fm**.

1. Locate the following rules:

   | Wrap this object or objects | In this element | With this qualifier |
   |---|---|---|
   | P:TableTitle | TableTitle | |
   | P:Pname | Pname | |
   | P:Pnum | Pnum | |
   | P:Pcount | Pcount | |
   | T:Format A | FormatA | |

   Because you are not allowing elements within the TableTitle, just <TEXT>, you do not need a rule for wrapping the P:TableTitle in an element.

   Because you are not allowing elements within the cells of the table, just <TEXT>, you do not need a rule for wrapping the cells' paragraphs in elements before wrapping them in table cell elements.

   For these reasons, delete the following rules:

   | P:TableTitle | TableTitle |
   |---|---|
   | P:Pname | Pname |
   | P:Pnum | Pnum |
   | P:Pcount | Pcount |

2. Table elements should use Table. Adding the word "(promote)" makes them a sibling, rather than a child, of the paragraph element in which they are anchored.

   For this reason, rewrite this rule as follows:

   | T:Format A | Table (promote) |
   |---|---|

3. Locate the following rules:

   | Wrap this object or objects | In this element | With this qualifier |
   |---|---|---|
   | TT: | TITLE | |
   | TH: | HEADING | |
   | TB: | BODY | |
   | TF: | FOOTING | |
   | TR: | ROW | |
   | TC: | CELL | |

These generic elements are already defined specifically in your EDD, so rewrite the rules for the table heading, table body, and table footing elements as follows:

| TH: | TableHeading |
|---|---|
| TB: | TableBody |
| TF: | TableFooting |

4. Rewrite the table row rule as follows to match the EDD:

| TR: | TableRow |
|---|---|

5. The content (using the Pname format) in the cell will be wrapped directly in the table cell element with the tag Name, so rewrite the table cell rule as follows to match the EDD:

| TC:P:Pname | Name |
|---|---|

6. The paragraph (using Pnum format) in the cell will be wrapped directly in the table cell element with the element tag PartNum. Pcount will be wrapped in Count, so add the following two rules:

| TC:P:Pnum | PartNum |
|---|---|
| TC:P:Pcount | Count |

7. Save your changes.

## Exercise 10: Wrapping Captions and Graphics in Figures

In this exercise, you will add a rule to group the Caption and Graphic together in a Figure element.

Although your EDD requires the Caption, you will make it optional in the wrapping process. In case an author forgot the Caption, Graphic will still be wrapped in Figure, with a square hole displaying in the **Structure View** where the Caption is missing.

Your goal is to wrap as much as possible, even if the unstructured document does not quite conform to the element definitions defined in the EDD.

In the end, you will have less manual wrapping to do.

1. Add the following rule:

| Wrap this object or objects | In this element | With this qualifier |
|---|---|---|
| E:Caption?, E:Graphic | Figure | |

2. Save your changes.

## Exercise 11: Wrapping Paras in Items in Lists

In this exercise, you will add several rules to wrap the various **Para** elements (by qualifier) in **Item**. Then, you will wrap the **Item** in a **List**.

1. Create rules for the following content that wraps in **Item**:

   The first rule wraps a **Para** with qualifier **Step1**—followed by zero or more of **Para** with qualifier **Substep**, **WarnNote**, and **Figure** elements—in an **Item** with qualifier **First**.

   The second rule wraps a **Para** with qualifier **Step**—followed by zero or more of **Para** with qualifier **Substep**, **WarnNote**, and **Figure** elements—in an **Item** with qualifier **Additional**.

   The third rule wraps a **Para** with qualifier **Bull**—followed by zero or more of **Para** with qualifier **Substep**, **WarnNote**, and **Figure** elements—in an **Item** with qualifier **BullItem** (watch the spelling).

   Add the following three rules:

   | Wrap this object or objects | In this element | With this qualifier |
   |---|---|---|
   | E:Para[Step1], (E:Para[Substep] \| E:WarnNote \| E:Figure)* | Item | First |
   | E:Para[Step], (E:Para[Substep] \| E:WarnNote \| E:Figure)* | Item | Additional |
   | E:Para[Bull], (E:Para[Substep] \| E:WarnNote \| E:Figure)* | Item | BullItem |

2. Create rules for the following content that wraps in **List**:

   The first rule wraps one or more **Item** elements with qualifier **BullItem** in a **List** with the **ListType** attribute and a value of **Bulleted**, which drives the formatting of bulleted lists in your EDD.

   The second rule wraps one **Item** element with qualifier **First**—followed by zero or more **Item** elements with qualifier **Additional**—in a **List** with the **ListType** attribute and a value of **Numbered**, which drives the formatting of numbered lists in your EDD.

   Again, to maximize the amount of automatic wrapping, the conversion rules for the number of items in a list can be less restrictive than the actual rules in the EDD. (EDD requires two, conversion rules require only one.) Missing required elements will display as square holes in the **Structure View**.

   Add the following two rules:

   | Wrap this object or objects | In this element | With this qualifier |
   |---|---|---|
   | E:Item[BullItem]+ | List [ListType = "Bulleted"] | |
   | E:Item[First], E:Item[Additional]* | List [ListType = "Numbered"] | |

3. Save your changes.

## Exercise 12: Wrapping Heads and Their Siblings in Sections

In this exercise, you will add several rules to wrap the various **Head** elements (by qualifier) and their siblings in a **Section**.

Create rules for the following content that wraps in **Section**:

The first rule wraps a 3rd-level **Head** and its siblings in a **Section** with qualifier **Section3**.

The second rule wraps a 2nd-level **Head** and its siblings (some of which can be a 3rd-level **Section**) in a **Section** with qualifier **Section2**.

The third rule wraps a 1st-level **Head** and its siblings (some of which can be a 2nd-level **Section**) in a **Section** with qualifier **Section1**.

Again, to maximize the amount of automatic wrapping, the conversion rules for the number of a subordinate-level **Section** within a parent **Section** are less restrictive than those in the EDD.

Add the following three rules:

| Wrap this object or objects | In this element | With this qualifier |
|---|---|---|
| E:Head[SH3], (E:Para[Regular] \| E:List \| E:Table \| E:Figure \| E:EQ \| E:WarnNote)+ | Section | Section3 |
| E:Head[SH2], (E:Para[Regular] \| E:List \| E:Table \| E:Figure \| E:EQ \| E:WarnNote \| Section[Section3])+ | Section | Section2 |
| E:Head[SH1], (E:Para[Regular] \| E:List \| E:Table \| E:Figure \| E:EQ \| E:WarnNote \| Section[Section2])+ | Section | Section1 |

1. Save your changes.

## Exercise 13: Wrapping the Highest-Level Element

In this exercise, you will add a final rule to wrap up the entire document in a **Chapter**.

To maximize the amount of automatic wrapping, the conversion rule doesn't require more than one **Section** in the **Chapter**. As long as you import element definitions from a structured template or EDD in the document you are wrapping, missing and misplaced elements will be found when validating.

1. Add the following rule:

    | | |
    |---|---|
    | E:Title, E:Section[Section1]+ | Chapter |

2. Save your changes.

## Completed Conversion Table

| Wrap this object or objects | In this element | With this qualifier |
|---|---|---|
| P:Title | Title | |
| P:H1 | Head | SH1 |
| P:H2 | Head | SH2 |
| P:H3 | Head | SH3 |
| P:Regular | Para | Regular |
| P:Bulleted | Para | Bull |
| P:Caption | Caption | |
| P:Indented | Para | Substep |
| P:StepFirst | Para | Step1 |
| P:Step | Para | Step |
| P:Note | WarnNote | |
| C:Emphasis | WarnNote | |
| X:ElemNumTextPage | XRef | |
| M:Index | IndexEntry | |
| Q: | EQ | |
| G: | Graphic (promote) | |
| F:flow | Footnote | |
| F:table | Footnote | |
| T:Format A | Table (promote) | |
| TT: | TableTitle | |
| TH: | TableHeading | |
| TB: | TableBody | |
| TF: | TableFooting | |
| TR: | TableRow | |
| TC:P:Pname | Name | |
| TC:P:Pnum | PartNum | |
| TC:P:Pcount | Count | |

| Wrap this object or objects | In this element | With this qualifier |
|---|---|---|
| E:Caption, E:Graphic | Figure | |
| E:Para[Step1], (E:Para[Substep] \| E:WarnNote \| E:Figure)* | Item | First |
| E:Para[Step], (E:Para[Substep] \| E:WarnNote \| E:Figure)* | Item | Additional |
| E:Para[Bull], (E:Para[Substep] \| E:WarnNote \| E:Figure)* | Item | BullItem |
| E:Item[BullItem]+ | List [ListType = "Bulleted"] | |
| E:Item[First], E:Item[Additional]* | List [ListType = "Numbered"] | |
| E:Head[SH3], (E:Para[Regular] \| E:List \| E:Table \| E:Figure \| E:EQ \| E:WarnNote)+ | Section | Section3 |
| E:Head[SH2], (E:Para[Regular] \| E:List \| E:Table \| E:Figure \| E:EQ \| E:WarnNote \| Section[Section3])+ | Section | Section2 |
| E:Head[SH1], (E:Para[Regular] \| E:List \| E:Table \| E:Figure \| E:EQ \| E:WarnNote \| Section[Section2])+ | Section | Section1 |
| E:Title, E:Section[Section1]+ | Chapter | |

## Structuring Unstructured Documents

With a conversion table, you can structure:

- Single files
- Groups of files
- Books and their component files

### Exercise 14: Structuring Current Unstructured Document

In this exercise, you will structure a single file using your conversion table.

1. If not still open, from your class files directory, open **Conversion Table.fm**.

    If you did not finish the conversion table, please open **Final Conversion Table.fm Conversion Table.fm** instead, and save it in your class files directory as **Conversion Table.fm**.

> If you have difficulty with the table you created, the **Final Conversion Table.fm** document can help you troubleshoot your conversion rules to find typos or mistakes.

2. From your class files directory, open **Final EDD.fm**.

> **Final EDD.fm** has slight structural differences from the EDD you finished up developing in the last chapter. Use **Final EDD.fm** and not **EDD.fm** for best results.

3. If not still open, from your class files directory, open **wraptest.fm**.

4. In **wraptest.fm**, import element definitions from **Final EDD.fm**
   a. From the **File** menu in `wraptest.fm`, choose **Import > Element Definitions**.
   b. From the **Import from Document** popup menu, choose **Final EDD.fm**.
   c. Click **Import**.

      An alert box appears indicating "**Element definitions have been imported from the EDD**"
   d. Click **OK** to close any alerts.
5. Save your changes.

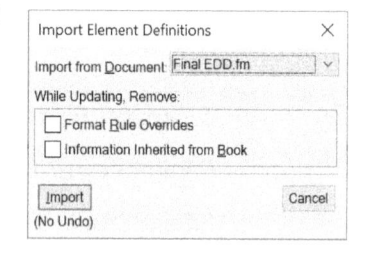

> By importing your EDD into the document to be structured, you are passing the EDD into your converted document. This may be significant in your own work, as you'll likely have many iterations of testing, and importing the EDD into each resulting converted document can become tedious.

6. From the **Structure** menu in **wraptest.fm**, choose **Utilities > Structure Current Document**.

   The **Structure Current Document** dialog appears
7. From the **Conversion Table Document** popup menu, choose **Conversion Table.fm**. (Choose Final Conversion Table.fm, if you didn't earlier complete your own conversion table.)
8. Click **Add Structure**.

   An alert appears indicating "**Operation completed normally.**"
9. Click **OK** to dismiss the alert.

   If there were errors, a log file appears diagnosing the errors.
10. If necessary, modify **Conversion Table.fm** and repeat the conversion.

    A new **NoName** document appears with the initial file's contents wrapped according to the rules in the conversion table.
11. Save the file as `wraptest.out.fm`.
12. Validate and correct any validation errors.

    You will need to correct a missing attribute value for the **Author** attribute and fix some unresolved cross-references, relinking them to **Table** and **Figure** elements, rather than paragraphs.
13. If elements do not appear to be wrapped correctly, modify **Conversion Table.fm** and restructure the **wraptest.fm** file, not the output file which is already wrapped.
14. Save and close all your files.

# Need FrameMaker Training?

## Train with Tech Comm Tools

### High Value
Each course has all of the content from my 100% live classes, along with an ever-growing library of in-depth material I've created in response to individual student needs.

### Easy to access
Each week you'll have live reviews, recorded lessons for key features, and relevant exercises. Can't make a live session? They're all recorded, so you review at your convenience.

### In-Depth
Honestly, you wouldn't want this much content in a 2-day class! But topics are marked as either CORE or TARGETED to let you get what you need without spending time on features that don't apply to your work.

Visit bit.ly/tc2ls-courses to see course schedule and syllabi

# TC 2LS Tech Comm Tools

- Live Training
- Online courses
- Dev/Consult

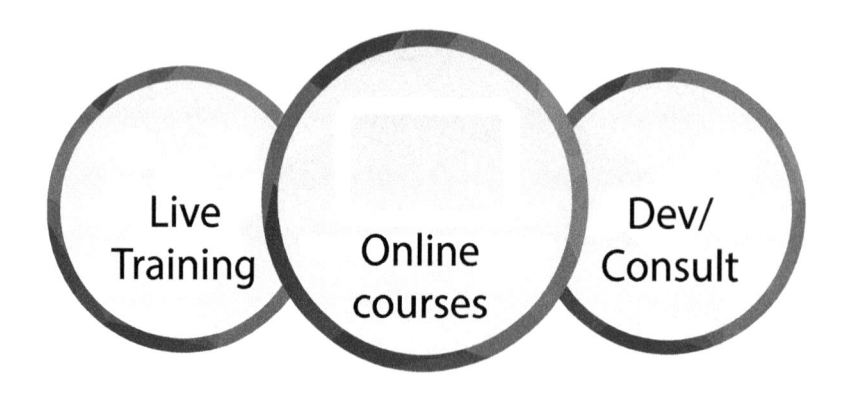

## Dig in as deep as you need

Whether it's an in-depth online course, a live training class, or just a quick solution for a specific problem, Tech Comm Tools has you covered! I've been providing Adobe certified training for over 20 years, and I provide all types of structured and unstructured FrameMaker courses.

## Course development and production

I produce video directly for Adobe and for my online courses, so I also have a great course on screencasting, or tech comm video. Ask me for a walkthrough of any of my courses.

### Fm Author
Learn how to create and edit content with FrameMaker. This course includes great info on HTML5 publishing along with books, graphics, cross-references, and table structures.

### Fm Templates
Join us for our flagship course...a six week collaborative project, where we create a polished working template for you and your organization

### Fm Structure
We have two structured FrameMaker courses, Authoring (for those new to structure), and EDD Develpment (for template designers). Ask to see our 2017 Structured Authoring workbook.

### Screen Casts
Creating video is easy, when you have the right plan. See how quickly you can produce quality video for use in training, support, website, and documentation.

### Quick Fixes
Sometimes you don't need training, you just need to get small things fixed...The next time you need to solve a small issue, visit bit.ly/short-consult

SCAN THIS CODE & I'LL PAY FOR YOUR BOOK*
*For $50 off any course visit bit.ly/coupon-50

www.techcomm.tools
info@techcomm.tools
714.585.2335